CONTENTS

v

INTRODUCTION

THOMAS ADAMS, a Selection from whose Sermons is here given, was an English divine of the 17th Century whom Southey pronounced to be the 'prose Shakespeare of Puritan theologians ......scarcely inferior to Fuller in wit or to Taylor in fancy.' Another eminent writer, of later date, claims for Adams that 'he stands in the forefront of our great English preachers, and while not so sustained as Jeremy Taylor, nor so continuously sparkling as Thomas Fuller, is yet surpassingly eloquent and brilliant, and much more thought-laden than either.'

Our earliest personal knowledge of this Puritan preacher is derived from the title-page of one of his sermons published in 1612, which describes him as 'a preacher of the Gospel at Willington' which is a rural parish in Bedfordshire, four miles east of Bedford town. The neighbourhood of Willington vicarage was not even then without some literary associations of its own. For two miles away stands the pleasant village of Cardington where in 1525 George

THE SERMONS OF
THOMAS ADAMS

THE
SHAKESPEARE OF PURITAN
THEOLOGIANS

THE SERMONS OF
THOMAS ADAMS

THE
SHAKESPEARE OF PURITAN
THEOLOGIANS

A SELECTION EDITED BY

JOHN BROWN, D.D.

CAMBRIDGE UNIVERSITY PRESS
Cambridge, New York, Melbourne, Madrid, Cape Town,
Singapore, São Paulo, Delhi, Mexico City

Cambridge University Press
The Edinburgh Building, Cambridge CB2 8RU, UK

Published in the United States of America by Cambridge University Press, New York

www.cambridge.org
Information on this title: www.cambridge.org/9781107668553

First published 1909
First paperback edition 2013

A catalogue record for this publication is available from the British Library

ISBN 978-1-107-66855-3 Paperback

INTRODUCTION

Gascoigne was born, our earliest English satirist, and one of the earliest of our strictly vernacular poets. He too has had his name connected with that of Shakespeare, for it has been said that the *Winter's Tale* was in part suggested by the joint version of the *Phenissae* by Gascoigne and Kinwelmersh ; and Gascoigne's *Steele Glas* may be said to be Shakespeare's 'Mirror held up to Nature' before Shakespeare's time—a 'glasse wherein each man may see within his mind what canckred vices be.' Again, coming to a later time, just across the Cardington border, in the East Fields of the parish of Elstow, stood the wayside cottage where in 1628 John Bunyan was born ; and a mile away to the south was Cople Wood End, where Samuel Butler formed part of the household of Sir Samuel Luke and where he wrote his *Hudibras*.

On leaving Willington, Thomas Adams became till 1636 Vicar of Wingrave, Bucks, and during the years he was there he seems also to have held the preachership of St Gregory's under St Paul's Cathedral, and was also Occasional Preacher at Paul's Cross and at Whitehall. In addition to these appointments he was 'Observant Chaplain' to Sir Henrie Montague, Lord Chief Justice of England. From the Epistles Dedicatory to his various works we gather that Adams lived on

vii

friendliest and most intimate terms with some of the foremost men in State and Church. William, Earl of Pembroke, Sir Thomas Egerton, Lord Ellesmere, and other men of rank are addressed by him as personal friends rather than as nobles and patrons.

A collection in one volume folio of Adams's Works, edited by himself was printed 'for John Grismond and sold at his shop in Ivie Lane at the sign of the Gunne, 1629.'

J. B.

April, 1909

THE CITY OF PEACE

*Live in peace; and the God of love and peace
shall be with you.*—2 Cor. xiii. 11.

PEACE is the daughter of righteousness, and
the mother of knowledge ; the nurse of arts, and
the improvement of all blessings.   It is delectable
to all that taste it, profitable to them that practise
it ; to them that look upon it, amiable ; to them
that enjoy it, a benefit invaluable.   The building
of Christianity knows no other materials.   If we
look upon the church itself, 'there is one body';
if upon the very soul of it, 'there is one Spirit';
if upon the endowment of it, 'there is one hope' ;
if upon the head of it, 'there is one Lord'; if
upon the life of it, 'there is one faith'; if upon
the door of it, 'there is one baptism'; if upon
the Father of it, 'there is one God, and Father of
all,' Eph. iv. 4.

Peace is a fair virgin, every one's love, the
praise of all tongues, the object of all eyes, the
wish of all hearts. She hath a smiling look,
which never frowned with the least scowl of

anger; snowy arms, soft as down, and whiter than the swan's feathers, always open to pious embracements. Her milken hand carries an olive branch, the symbol and emblem of quietness. She hath the face of a glorious angel, always looking towards righteousness, as the two cherubims looked one upon the other, and both unto the mercy-seat. Her court is the invincible fort of integrity; so guarded by the divine providence, that drums, trumpets, and thundering cannons, those loud instruments of war, (I mean blasphemy, contention, violence,) may affront her, but never affright her. She hath a bounteous hand, virtual like the garment of Christ; if a faithful soul can come to touch it, to kiss it, all her vexations are fled, her conscience is at rest. Her bowels are full of pity; she is always composing salves for all the wounds of a broken heart. Sedition and tumult her very soul hates; she tramples injuries and discords under her triumphant feet. She sits in a throne of joy, and wears a crown of eternity; and to all those that open the door of their heart to bid her welcome, she will open the door of heaven to bid them welcome, and repose their souls in everlasting peace. In these continual dog-days of ours, wherein love waxeth cold, and strife hot, we had need set our instruments to the tune of peace. This was the

2

blessed legacy which Christ bequeathed to his church ; the Apostle from his Master sent it as a token to the Corinthians ; and I from the Apostle commend it as a jewel to all Christians : ' Live in peace; and the God of love and peace shall be with you.' Which conclusion of the epistle contains the blessing of the Apostle ; a valediction, and a benediction. They are in part hortatory, in part consolatory ; the virtue to which he persuades them, and the reward which he promiseth them. There is a sweet symphony and respondent proportion between the counsel and the comfort, the active peace and the factive peace : for seeking peace on earth, we shall find peace in heaven ; for keeping the peace of God, we shall be kept by the God of peace. The one is the regular compass of our life on earth, the other is the glorious crown of our life in heaven.

Some have a good mind to peace, but they will be at no labour about it ; many are content to embrace it, but they are ashamed to seek it ; most men love it, few practise it. The use commends the virtue : the beauty and praise of peace consists not in motion, but in action ; nor is the benefit of it in a knowing discourse, but in a feeling sense. A speculative peace is like an historical knowledge, such as he that hath been always confined to his study may have

3   1—2

of foreign countries. So we make a conquest of peace, as the byword says our fathers won Boulogne ; who never came within the report of the cannon. Or as the Grecians kept philosophy in their leaves, but kept it not in their lives. A jejune and empty speculation, like some subtle air in the head, only breaks out into crotchets : it is experience that brings the sweetness of peace home to the heart. Use breeds perfectness, and disuse loseth the most serviceable things. Gold loseth more of its weight by rusting in corners, than by continual running in commerces, the proper end it was coined for. The best land will yield small increase if it be not tilled ; though some have the most profitable trades, the want of industry hath made them the poorest men. The throne of peace is in the heart, not in the head.

To recover, therefore, the swooning life of this virtue, I will compare peace to a city : if you will, to this city ; which should be, like Jerusalem, a 'city of peace.' And so much we will pray for it : that it may preserve peace, and peace may preserve it, to the world's end.

I. Let the walls of this city be unity and concord. II. Let her have four gates : innocence and patience, benefaction and satisfaction. The first gate of peace is innocence ; she must do no wrong. The second is patience ; she must suffer

4

wrong. The third is beneficence ; she must do good instead of wrong. The fourth is recompense ; she must make liberal and just satisfaction for any committed wrong. There is also a postern gate, and that is humility : a gate indeed, but a small and low one ; whosoever enters the city of peace that way, must stoop before he get in. III. The enemies of this city are many, divided into two bands—hostility and mutiny. IV. The government of it is magistracy. V. The law, religion. VI. The palace, the temple. VII. It is served by the river of prosperity. VIII. The life of the citizens is love. IX. The state of it is felicity. X. The inheritance, eternal glory.

I. The walls of peace are unity and concord. *Omnis societas est corpus politicum ;* and it is in a city as in a body : there are many members, one body ; many citizens, one city. The body is one of the most lively figures and examples of peace. 'We are all one body,' i Cor. xii. Not only one kingdom ; so disparity in religions makes many differences. Nor only one city ; so disparity of estates will breed quarrels. Nor only one house ; so we may have 'enemies of our own household.' But one body, here must be all love and peace. Where all are tied by bonds, joints, and ligaments to the head ; there also by the same nerves one to another.

5

Some members are single : as the tongue is one, to speak one truth ; the heart one, to entertain one God.   Other are *gemina, germana ;* their forces are doubled to supply mutual defects. Some are stronger, as the arms and legs, for the supportation of the weaker.   Thus qualified are all the faithful citizens of peace ; preserving a unanimity in affection, a sympathy in affliction, a ready help to the most needful condition ; comforting the minds of those that are perplexed, supplying the wants of those that are distressed, rectifying the weakness of those that are unsettled, informing the ignorance of those that are seduced, and reforming the errors of those that are perverted : all endeavouring the deliverance of the oppressed.

The members provide one for another : the eye sees not for itself, but for the body ; the hand works not only for itself, but for the body ; the ear hearkens, the tongue talks, the foot walks, all parts exercise their functions for the good of the whole.

If one member suffer, the rest suffer with it. If there be a thorn in the foot, the eye sheds a tear, the heart aches, the head grieves, the hand is ready to pull it out.

The walls of the city must be whole, no breaches in them, lest this advantage the enemy's entrance.

There must be no schism in a city, as no division
in the body : one must not be for Paul, another
for Apollos, another for Cephas ; but all for
Christ, and all for peace. Many evil men may
have one will in wickedness. It is said of Pilate,
Luke xxiii. 25, *Tradidit Jesum voluntati eorum,*—
' He delivered Jesus to their will,' not wills ; many
sinners, one will. Shall, then, the sons of grace
jar ? the children of peace be mutinous ? Saith
Christ,—' My dove is but one.' The dove is a
bird of peace : many of them can agree lovingly
together in one house ; every one hath a little
cottage by herself, wherein she sits content,
without disquieting her neighbours. Thus *dum
singulæ quærunt unionem, omnes conservant
unitatem.* We have them that rush into others'
tabernacles, swallowing a man and his heritages :
would doves do thus ? Poor Naboth's portion is
many a rich Ahab's eye-sore : would doves do
thus ? Numbers are still on the wing to prey
upon prostrate fortunes ; these be ravens, not
doves. If the law cannot make work for their
malice, their malice shall make work for the
law. This is like cocks of the game, to peck out
one another's eyes to make the lawyers sport.
When two friends are fallen out of love into blows,
and are fighting, a third adversary hath a fair
advantage to kill them both. We have an enemy

that watcheth his time, and while we wound one another, he wounds us all.

II. So I come from the walls to the gates.

1. The first gate is innocence; and this may be called *Bishopsgate*, the ministers of the gospel being both the preachers and precedents of innocency. If men would abstain from doing wrong, the peace could not be broken. St Bernard writes of the dove, that she hath no gall. Let us be such doves, to purge our hearts from all bitterness.

Now the first shelf that wrecks innocence is anger. It were rare if 'the wrath of man should fulfil the righteousness of God'; even a curst anger breaks the peace. It is an evidence whereby God will judge men guilty: now there is no malefactor going to the bar for his trial would willingly have that evidence found about him that should cast him. The wrathful man takes no notice of the law, but the law takes notice of the wrathful man. Let us take heed lest we carry our anger with us unto God.

2. The second gate is patience, which is not unlike to *Ludgate;* for that is a school of patience, the poor souls there learn to suffer. The first entrance of peace is to do no injury, the next is to suffer injury. It is one special commendation of charity, that it 'suffers all things.' For our brethren

we must sustain some loss : he that suffers not an abatement of his own fulness to supply their emptiness, is no brother. Of our brethren we must put up some wrong, rather than make a flaw in the smooth passage of peace.

According to the Apostle's counsel, ' Let us bear the burden one of another,' and God shall bear the burden of us all. As in the arch of a building, one stone bears mutually, though not equally, the weight of the rest. Or as deer swimming over a great water do ease themselves in laying their heads one upon the back of another ; the foremost having none to support him, changeth his place and rests his head upon the hindmost. Bear thou with his curiousness, he doth bear with thy furiousness ; let me bear with his arrogance, he doth bear with my ignorance. The Italians have a proverb, ' Hard without soft, the wall is nought.' Stones cobbled up together, without mortar to combine them, make but a tottering wall. But if there be mortar to cement them, and with the tractable softness of the one to glue and fix the solid hardness of the other, this may fortify it against the shock of the ram or shot of the cannon. The society that consists of nothing but stones, intractable and refractory spirits, one as froward and perverse as another, soon dissolves. But when one is reeking

9

with the fire of rage, and another shall bring the water of patience to cool and quench it, here is a duration of peace. When iron meets iron, there is a harsh and stubborn jar; let wool meet that rougher metal, and this yielding turns resistance into embracements.

3. The next gate is beneficence. Doing good is the fortification of peace. This may be called *Aldgate;* not only because there is the picture of Charity at the gate,—I do not say, as near going out, but at the gate, to keep goodness in,—but because that is called the *Old-gate*, and charity was a virtue of old times, not so much now in fashion. The gospel chargeth us, 'while we have opportunity, to do good to all men'; albeit with some preferment of the best, 'especially to the household of faith,' Gal. vi. 10.

All men may be ranked under one of these combinations: rich and poor, home-born and strangers, friends and enemies.

First, for the rich and poor. The Pharisee will stand on good terms with the rich, invite them for a re-invitation; as men at tennis toss the ball to another, that he may toss it to them again. But who helps the poor? 'Wealth maketh many friends, but the poor is separated from his neighbour,' Prov. xix. 4. If he do well, he is not regarded; if ill, he is destroyed.

For domestics and strangers. Many have so much religion as to provide for their own, yea, so much irreligion as to do it with the prejudice of the public good and hazard of their own souls : but who provides for strangers? 'Entertain strangers ; for thereby some have entertained angels unawares,' Heb. xiii. 2. But for all this possible happiness, few will put it to the venture : and were they indeed angels, without angels in their purses to pay for it, they should find cold entertainment.

Friends and enemies. For friends, many will be at peace with them, till they be put to the trial by some expressive action ; and then they will rather hazard the loss of a friend than the least loss by a friend. But suppose we answer our friends in some slight courtesy, hoping for a greater, who will do good to his enemies? 'If thine enemy hunger, feed him : so thou shalt heap coals of fire on his head,' Rom. xii. 20. Do it, not with an intent to make his reckoning more, but thy own reckoning less.

4. The fourth gate is recompense, or satisfaction ; and this we may liken to *Cripplegate*. It is the lamest way to peace, yet a way : it is a halting gate, but a gate. It were far better coming into this city by any of the former gates, yet better at this than none. All come not by

innocence, nor all by patience, nor all by beneficence; but if they have failed in these, they
must be admitted by recompense, or not at all.
The first best is to do no injury; the next is
satisfaction, to make amends for that we have
done. Hortensius said of his mother, I never
was reconciled to her, because we two never fell
out. Oh that the inhabitants of this city could
say so of their neighbours : We never were made
friends, because we never were foes ! But as our
Saviour saith, 'It is necessary that offences do
come': not that it should be so, but that it will
be so. There is no necessity that compels a man
to sin ; except that the heart being evil, will give
offence. As it is necessary for him that comes
to the fire to be made hot; but there is no
necessity that he come unto the fire.

The malady of offences will be contracted,
therefore the only cure is by satisfaction. That
we may know how to do this, the Scripture sets
down divers degrees in the accomplishment of this
satisfaction for injuries. First, He must go to the
party wronged. Secondly, He must confess
his fault. Thirdly, He must humble himself.
Fourthly, He must make restitution. Fifthly, He
must reconcile himself. Sixthly, And this must
be done quickly, with all possible speed.

  5. These be the main gates ; there is a little

postern besides, that is, humility : for of all vices, pride is a stranger to peace. The proud man is too guilty, to come in by innocence ; too surly, to come in by patience : he hath no mind to come in by benefaction ; and he scorns to come in by satisfaction. All these portcullises be shut against him : there is no way left but the postern for him ; he must stoop, or never be admitted to peace. Pride is always envious and contumelious, thinking she adds so much to her own reputation as she detracts from others : she is no fit neighbour for peace.

Heaven is a high city, yet hath but a low gate. —Take away pride, and that which thou hast is mine ; take away envy, and that which I have is thine. Pride and envy are too uncivil for a peaceable city : the one cannot endure a vicine prosperity, nor the other a superior eminency. All men must be poor to please the one, and all must be base to content the other. Peace is humble, pride quite overlooks her. The philosopher might have seen the stars in the water ; he could not see the water in the stars when he stumbled into the ditch. Men may behold glory in humility, they shall never find peace in ambition. The safest way to keep fire is to rake it up in embers ; the best means to preserve peace is in humbleness. The tall cedars feel the fury of tempests, which blow over the humble shrubs in the low valleys. There was no rule with Paul at first; raising tumults, speeding commissions, breathing out slaughters against poor Christians; but when Christ had thundered him from his horse, broken his wild spirit to humility, then he was fit for peace. God, that often effectuates his own will by contraries, makes trouble the preparation for peace; as a father corrects his unruly children that they may be quiet. Let us examine our own experience: when the Lord hath soundly scourged us, we go from under his fingers as tame as lambs; farewell strife, all our care is to find rest and peace in Jesus Christ.

III. We have seen the city of peace, with her walls and gates, and we wish well to her: 'Peace be within thy walls, and prosperity within thy palaces,' Ps. cxxii. 7. But hath she no adversaries? Yes; there is an enemy that beleaguers this city—contention; whose army is divided into two bands or troops: the one called the civil, the other the uncivil; the civil are law quarrels, the uncivil are sword quarrels. The one is the smoothfaced company, the other the rugged or ragged regiment. The city of peace hath gates for these also, when she hath subdued them. Either she turns them out at *Moorgate*, as fitter

for the society of Moors and pagans—she banish-
eth them ; or lays them up in *Newgate*—a place
very convenient, being not so old as peace, built
since the birth of strife. These enemies pursue
us, *vel ferro, vel foro,* as that father saith.

Ferro ; when upon every punctilio of honour,
as they falsely call it, reason and religion must be
thrown by, and fury govern. The gallant, as if
he knew no law but his own will, or as if the least
aspersion upon his honour were more weighty
than if the state of Christendom or the glory of
God lay upon it, cries, Revenge ! offers the stab,
threatens the pistol.

Foro ; there is another battalia of adversaries
that turn their challenge into a writ : the field
appointed is Westminster Hall or some other
court of justice ; the weapons, the law ; the
postures of the fight are demurs, delays, quirks,
removals ; the victory, a verdict ; the doom, a
sentence ; and the death itself, an execution.
One says, To bear this is against my conscience ;
when indeed he means it is against his concupiscence. If the plaintiff go no further than the
court of his own affections, the defendant shall
never have audience ; for he is *amicus curiæ.*
'He that is first in his own cause seemeth just ;
but his neighbour cometh and searcheth him.'
Lawyers first invented laws to secure our lands

and titles ; now they make those laws engines to get away our lands and titles. Their frequent session hath not been evermore to preserve a man's possession. And for those that can tarry the leisure of the law, they have quirks and delays. And what doth the winner get, that at the term's end he may brag of his gains ? Doth he not come home dry-foundered ? Doth he not follow the mill so long, till the toll be more than the grist ? It is a token of unwholesome air, where the country is full of thriving physicians. It argues little health in that kingdom which hath so many thriving lawyers ; who while unquietness feeds us, do quietly feed upon us.

In the race of Christianity, there is a contrary law of striving : not he that offers most blows, but he that suffers most blows, is crowned. A man is stricken ; will he go to law for this? No, rather let him turn the other cheek ; this is Christ's counsel. His clóak is taken from him : it is near him, a garment ; of necessary comeliness, a cloak ; of singular use, he hath but one cloak ; he hath the propriety of it, it is his cloak : must he go to law for this? No, rather let him take his coat also.

IV. The governor of this city is supreme authority. As God is a great King, so the king is, as it were, a little god. ' I have said, Ye are gods.' God is an invisible King, the king is a visible god. 'Ye must be subject, not only for wrath, but also for conscience sake,' Rom. xiii. 5. All must obey: the bad for fear, the good for love. To compel the one, there is a writ out of the King's Bench; to persuade the other, there is an order in the Chancery.

Anarchy is the mother of division, the step-mother of peace. While the state of Italy wants a king, all runs into civil broils. It is the happiness of this city that there is no distraction. Not a king at Judah, and another at Dan; not one in Hebron, another in Gibeon; not the red rose here, and the white there. We are not shuffled into a popular government, nor cut into cantons by a headless, headstrong aristocracy; but *Henricus Rosas, Regna Jacobus*,—in Henry was the union of the roses, in James of the kingdoms. Every king is not a peacemaker: ours, like a second Augustus, hath shut the rusty door of Janus's temple; so making peace, as if he were made of peace. That blessed queen, of sweet and sacred memory before him, was *Filia Pacis;* who, as by her sexual graces she deserved to be the queen of women, so by her masculine virtues to be the queen of men. Certainly, it would have troubled any king but him, to have succeeded such a queen; yet no man complains the want of peace.

This he promised, and this he hath performed to every good soul's content. When he was first proclaimed, what heard we but peace? What heard the nobles? a king that would honour them. What the senators? a king that would counsel them. What the schools? a king that would grace them. What the divines? a king that would encourage them. What the rich? a king that would defend them. What the poor? a king that would relieve them.

V. The law of this city is the law of Christ : a law indeed, but a law of peace. It made peace betwixt God and man ; and it must make peace between man and man. If it cannot reconcile us one to another, it shall reconcile none of us to the Lord. It is a law, not to be observed for state, but for conscience. This city of peace hath one immutable rule, and it is sufficient to direct all actions : 'And as many as walk according to this rule, peace be on them, and mercy, and upon the Israel of God,' Gal. vi. 16. A man is proud of his victorious mischiefs, fleshed with his fortunate wickedness, thinks he hath carried himself bravely in out-bribing his adversary, fooling judge and jury by false testimony, and triumphs in his unblest gain : but is this according to the rule of peace? Let truth overcome. The loser may sit down with content, but the winner shall lie down in torment. A rich man carries himself proudly; above others in scorn, above himself in folly : he thinks all his titles beneath him, and even those that worship him still to undervalue him; others he looks upon as if they were made to serve him, yea, and be proud to be commanded by him. Cross him, and he rages, swells, foams like the sea in a storm; but is this after the rule of peace? 'Learn of me, who am meek and lowly in heart.'

VI. The palace of peace is the temple : the peace of man can never be preserved without the worship of God. It is not enough for the city to have laws, but these must be divulged, made known to the inhabitants, the observation of them continually urged; for by nature men are apt enough to fly out. Howsoever the Romans built their *Templum Pacis* without the gates, yet here it is the chief honour and ornament of the city. Here Peace keeps her court, and sits like a royal queen in her chair of estate : which is not like Solomon's throne, guarded with lions, but with milk-white doves, and covered over with olive branches.

VII. The river that serves this city of peace is prosperity. It is one principal happiness of a city to be situated by a river's side : that as it hath fortified itself by land, so it may have command of the sea. Prosperity is the river to

this city, that like a loving Meander, winds itself
about, throwing his silver arms upon her sides;
ebbing slowly, but flowing merrily, as if he longed
to embrace his love. Peace is the mother of
prosperity, but prosperity is too often the murderer
of peace. For peace breeds wealth, wealth breeds
pride, pride breeds contention, and contention
kills peace. Thus she is often destroyed by her
own issue, as Sennacherib was by his own bowels.

Take this city we live in for an instance.
Peace hath brought God's plenty: the inhabitants
neither plough, nor sow, nor reap; yet are fed
like the fowls of heaven. They fare well with
less trouble than if corn grew at their doors, and
cattle grazed in their streets. But as Nilus may
rise too high, and water Egypt too much, so the
inundation of opulency may do them hurt. Thus
may the influence of heaven, and the plenty of
earth, be a snare unto us, and our abundance an
occasion of our falling. Prosperity is hearty
meat, but not digestible by a weak stomach;
strong wine, but naught for a weak brain. 'The
prosperity of fools destroyeth them,' Prov. i. 32.
It is not simply prosperity, but the prosperity of
fools, that destroyeth them. The swelling river
by the surfeit of a tide doth not sooner bring in
our increase, but our increase doth breed in our
mind another swelling, in our bodies another

surfeiting : we swell in pride, and surfeit in wantonness. The Israelites never fared so well as when they lived at God's immediate finding, and at night expected their morrow's breakfast from the clouds ; when they did daily ask, and daily receive, their daily bread.

There be (as I heard a worthy divine observe) three main rivers in the land, whereof this is held the best ; and this city is placed in the best seat of the river, upon the gentle rising of a hill, in the best air, and richest soil. When a courtier gave it out, that Queen Mary, being displeased with the city, threatened to divert both term and parliament to Oxford, an alderman asked whether she meant to turn the channel of the Thames thither or no : If not, saith he, by God's grace, we shall do well enough. 'The lines are fallen to us in pleasant places; we have a goodly heritage,' Ps. xvi. 6. Both the elements are our friends : the earth sends us in her fruits, the sea her merchandise. We are near enough the benefits, and far enough from the dangers, of the ocean. Nothing is wanting to the consummation of our happiness, to keep us in our own country, in our own city, in our own houses, but that which keeps men in their wits—temperance and thankfulness.

VIII. The life of the citizens is love : for

without the love of men there can be no peace of God ; and there is no love of God in them that desire not peace with men. He that loves not the members was never a friend to the Head. To say we love Christ, and hate a Christian, is as if a man, while he was saluting or protesting love to his friend, should tread on his toes. I know indeed that every creature is to be loved, but *in ordine ad Deum.* Religion doth not forbid, but rectify our affections. Our parents, spouses, children, allies, countrymen, neighbours, friends, have all their due places in our love ; and it were a brutish doctrine to dispossess us of these human relations. Only they must know their orders and stations, and by no means usurp upon God : they must not be mistresses, but handmaids to the love of Christ.

But let us love them because they love God : as reflections of our sight, which glance from the Lord upon his image. If God have their hearts, let them have our hearts. It is poor to love a man for that is about him : he must be loved for that is within him. If we should account of men as we do of bags, prize them that weigh heaviest ; and measure out our love by the subsidy-book, honouring a man because he is well clothed ; I see then no reason but we should do greater reverence to the bason and ewer on the stall, than to the goldsmith in the shop ; and most humbly salute satin and velvet in whole pieces, because their virgin-glory was never yet ravished and abused into fashion.

No, but especially let us love others, because they fear God, and serve Jesus Christ. For as the brain is to the sinews, the liver to the veins, and the heart to the arteries ; so is God's love to human societies : as the very soul by which they live, and the form that gives them being.

IX. Thus we have a real abridgment of this mystical city of peace ; happy every way. Vigilancy is her officer of peace, that hath an eye in the darkest angles, and discovers the first conceptions of strife. Discipline is her clerk of the peace, that keeps the records, and indicts offenders. Authority is her justice of peace, that if any will not be ruled, binds them over to the peace. Equity is her burse, where men exchange kindness for kindness ; on whose stairs injury and imposture durst never set their foul feet. Truth is her standard, which with the trumpet of fame shall resound her happiness to all nations. Plenty is her treasurer, liberality her almoner, conscience her chancellor, wisdom her counsellor, prayer her clerk of the closet, faith her crown, justice her sceptre, masculine virtues her peers, graces her attendants, and nobility her maid of honour. All

her garments are green and orient ; all her paths
be milk, her words oracles, and her works
miracles : making the blind to see, and the lame
to go, by a merciful supply to their defects.
Her breath is sweeter than the new-blown rose,
millions of souls lie sucking their life from it; and
the smell of her garments is like the smell of
Lebanon. Her smiles are more reviving than
the vertumnal sunshine ; and her favours, like
seasonable dews, spring up flowers and fruits
wheresoever she walks. Holiness is the canopy
of state over her head, and tranquillity the arras
where she sets her foot. All her servants wait
in order, and can with contentful knowledge
distinguish and accept their own places. Her
court is an image of paradise ; all her channels
flow with milk, and her conduits run wine. Envy
and murmuring, as privy to their own guilt, fly
from her presence. Her guard consists not of
men, but angels ; and they pitch their tents about
her palace.

X. Lastly, having preserved and blessed all her
children on earth, she goes with them to heaven,
is welcomed into the arms of her Father, invested
queen with a diadem of glory, and possessed of
those joys unto which time shall never put an
end.

THE FATAL BANQUET

*Stolen waters are sweet, and the bread of secrecies
is pleasant. But he knoweth not that the
dead are there; and that her guests are in
the depths of hell.*—Prov. ix. 17, 18.

I HAVE here chosen two texts in one, intending
to preach of a couple of preachers; one by
usurpation, the other by assignation : the world's
chaplain, and the Lord's prophet. The *sermons*
differ as well as the texts. (1) The harlot's *dixit*,
ver. 16, is thus amplified : 'Stolen waters are
sweet, and the bread of secrecies is pleasant.'
Tullius, nor Tertullus, nor Hermes, the speaker
in the parliament of the heathen gods, never
moved so eloquent a tongue.   She preaches,
according to the palate of her audience, *placentia ;*
nay, it is *placenta*, a sweet cake, whose flour is
sugar, and the humour that tempers it honey,
sweet, pleasant.   She cannot want auditors for
such a sermon ; for, as it is in fairs, the pedlar
and the balladmonger have more throng than the
rich merchant : Vanity hath as many customers

as she can turn to, when Verity hath but a cold
market. (2) Solomon's sermon is opposed to it
with a *but:* 'But he knoweth not that the dead
are there, and that her guests are in the depths
of hell.' A cross blow, that disarms the devil's
fencer; a flat conviction, or *non-plus*, given to
the arguments of sin; a little coloquintida put
into the sweet pot. That, as I have observed in
some beguiling pictures, look on it one way, and
it presents to you a beautiful damsel; go on the
adverse side, and behold it is a devil, or some mis-
shapen stigmatic : sin shews you a fair picture—
'Stolen waters are sweet,' &c., pleasure and
delight; Solomon takes you on the other side,
and shews you the ugly visages of death and
hell—'The dead are there,' &c. If sin open her
shop of delicacies, Solomon shews the trap-door
and the vault; if she boast her olives, he points
to the prickles ; if she discovers the green and gay
flowers of *delice*, he cries to the ingredients, The
serpent lurks there. She charms, and he breaks
her spells. As curious and proud as her house
is, Solomon is bold to write 'Lord, have mercy
on us,' on the doors, and to tell us the plague is
there : 'Stolen waters are sweet,' &c. ; 'but the
dead are there,' &c.

But allegorically sin is here shadowed by
the harlot; voluptuousness, the harlot of harlots,

whose bawd is Beelzebub, and whose bridewell is
broad hell. Wickedness is compared to a woman,
and hath all her senses : lust is her eye to see ;
injury, her hands to feel ; sensuality, her palate to
taste ; malice, her ears to hear ; petulancy, her nose
to smell ; and, because she is of the feminine sex,
we will allow her the sixth sense, tittle-tattle is
her tongue to talk. This is the common hostess
of the world, Satan's housekeeper, whose doors
are never shut. There is no man in the world
keeps such hospitality, for he searcheth the air,
earth, sea, nay, the kitchen of hell, to fit every
palate. Vitellius searched far and wide for the
rarities of nature, birds, beasts, fishes of inestim-
able price, which yet brought in, the bodies are
scorned, and only the eye of this bird, the tongue
of that fish, is taken, that the spoils of many
might be sacrifices to one supper. The emperor
of the low countries—hell—hath delicates of
strange variety, curiosity. Is any courtier proud?
Here are piles of silks. Is any officer troubled
with the itch in his hands? Here is *unguentum
aureum* to cure it ; a mess of bribes. Hath any
gentleman the hunger-worm of covetousness?
Here is cheer for his diet: usuries, oppressions,
exactions, enclosings, rackings, rakings, pleasing
gobbets of avarice. Is any tradesman light-
fingered and lighter-conscienced? Here is a

whole feast of frauds, a table furnished with
tricks, conveyances, glossings, perjuries, cheatings.
Hath any Papist a superstitious appetite? He is
set down in the chair of ignorance, and to him
are served in, by Sorbonnists, Jesuits, Seminaries,
Loyolists, a large and lavish feast of crucifixes,
unctions, scrapings, traditions, relics, &c.; and, as
cheese to digest all the rest, yet itself never digest-
ed, treason. For your rout of epicures, ruffians,
roarers, drunkards, boon companions, you may
know the place easily where these kestrels light,
even at the carcase-feast. Sin hath invited them,
and they scorn to be scornful. Hither they come,
and every man hath a dish by himself,—eat
whiles he blows again,—except their appetites
agree in the choice. You hear the inviter.

Let it not pass us without observation : Satan
is not without his factors abroad. He hath spirits
enough of his own,—'My name is legion,' Mark
v. 9,—but he is not content except he suborn man
against man.

He hath infinite petty stales to tempt men to
sin whom he hath officered for bidders to this
feast. Take a short muster of some of his inviters,
engineers, bidders to this banquet of Vanity;
they have all their separate stands.

(1) In the *Court* he hath set *Ambition* to
watch for base minds would stoop to any villany

for preferment, and to bring them to this feast. This attempt can tempt none but the base; the noble spirit cannot be so wrought upon. This is a principal bidder.

(2) In *Foro*, at the hall gates, he sets inviters, that beckon contention to them, and fill the world with broils. I mean neither the reverend judges, nor the worthy councillors, nor the good attorneys; but the libels of law—*Solicitors* indeed, for they are a solicitation to our peace; pettifoggers, Satan's firebands, and mortal things, which 'he casteth abroad to make himself sport.' But they do more hurt amongst the barley, the commons of this land, than Samson's foxes with the fire at their tails, Judges xv. 5. Oh that they were shipped out for Virginia, or, if they would trouble so good a soil, into some desert, where they might set beasts together by the ears, for they cannot live without making broils!

(3) *Pride* is another bidder, and keeps a shop in the *City*. You shall find a description of her shop, and take an inventory of her wares, from the prophet, Isa. iii., 'the tinkling ornaments, the cauls, and the moon-tires,' &c. She sits upon the stall, and courts the passengers with a *What lack ye?* Nay, besides her person, she hangs out her picture; a picture unlike herself, though she appears not unlike her picture—all paint. Infinite

traffic comes to her, but with the same luck and success that visitant beasts came to the sick lion— *vestigia nulla retrorsum;* or at best, as the runners to Rome, that return with shame and beggary.

(4) *Engrossing* is another inviter, and hath a large walk ; sometimes he watcheth the landing of a ship ; sometimes he turns whole loads of corn besides the market. This bidder prevails with many a citizen, gentleman, farmer, and brings in infinite guests ; the devil gives him a letter of mark for his piracy.

(5) *Bribery* is an officious fellow, and a special bidder to this feast. He invites both forward and froward : the forward and yielding, by promises of good cheer, that they shall have a fair day of it ; the backward honest man, by terrors and menaces that his cause shall else go westward (indeed, it goes to Westminster !). Yea, with pretence of commiseration and pity, as if the conscience of their right did animate him to their cause. Thus with a show of sanctimony they get a saint's money ; but indeed, there is no persuasion more pathetical than the purse's. Bribery stands at the stair-foot in the robes of an officer, and helps up injury to the place of audience ; thus Judas's bag is drawn with two strings, made of silk and silver, favour and reward.

All officers belong not to one court ; their

conditions alter with their places. There are some that seem so good that they lament the vices whereupon they yet inflict but pecuniary punishments. Some of them are like the Israelites, with a sword in one hand and a trowel in the other, with the motto of that old emblem, *In utrumque paratus;* as the one hand daubs up justice, so the other cuts breaches of division. They mourn for truth and equity, as the sons of Jacob for Joseph, when themselves sold it ; they exclaim against penal transgressions. So Caius Gracchus defends the treasury from others' violence, whiles himself robbed it ; so the poinder chafes and swears to see beasts in the corn, yet will pull up a stake, or cut a tether, to find supply for his pin-fold ; so Charles the Fifth was sorry for the Pope's durance, and gave orders of public prayers for his release, yet held him in his own hands prisoner.

(6) *Faction* keeps the *Church*, and invites some vain-glorious priests to this feast : schism and separation, like a couple of thorns, prick the Church's side, wound our mother till her heart bleeds.

(7) *Riot* is his inviter in a *tavern*. He sits like a young gallant at the upper end of the table, and drinks so many and so deep healths to the absent, that the present have no health left them.

31

This is a frequented inviting-place, that I say not the feast itself.

(8) *Oppression* hath a large circuit, and is a general bidder to the banquet. This factor hath abundance of the devil's work in hand: he untiles the houses of the poor, that whiles the storms of usury beat them out, he may have peaceable entrance; he joins house to house, as if he was straitened of room.

There are infinite swarms of inviters besides which run the Vagabonds on the devil's errand. All these declare to us the banquet's preparation. They are messengers of our wreck, porpoises prenourishing a tempest; usurers, brokers, vagrants, ruffians, blasphemers, tipplers, churls, wantons, pedlars of pernicious wares, seminaries, incendiaries, apostates, humorists, seditious troublers of our peace; you may perceive that our winter is busy by the flying abroad of these wild geese. All are bidders.

The junkets are prescribed, of what kind they are—*waters, bread.* They are described, of what property, virtue, nature—*stolen, secret.* They are ascribed to, of what operation, relish, or quality—*sweet, pleasant,* stolen waters, &c. Thus have you their quiddity, their quantity, their quality. This is the banquet, dainty and cherishing; cheap for it is stolen; delightful for it is sweet. We will ascend to view this feast, not to feed on it, by the stairs and degrees of my text.

First, *Waters.* Not the waters that the Spirit moved on at the creation ; nor the waters of regeneration, sanctifying waters ; nor the waters of Bethesda, stirred by an angel, salutary and medicinal ; nor the waters issuing from under the threshold of the sanctuary ; but the bitter waters of Marah, without the sweet word of grace to season them ; tumultuous waters ; waters of trouble ; waters of tribulation. These then are the *waters*: not the waters of regeneration, wherein our fathers and we have been baptized ; nor the waters of consolation, which 'make glad the city of God'; nor the waters of sanctification, wherein Christ once, the Spirit of Christ still, washeth the feet, the affections of the saints ; not the Hyblæan nectar of heaven, whereof he that drinks 'shall never thirst again,' John iv. 14 ; nor the waters of that 'pure river of life, clear as crystal, proceeding out of the throne of God,' Rev. xxii. 1 ; but the lutulent, spumy, maculatory waters of sin, either squeezed from the spongy clouds of our corrupt natures, or surging from the contagious (veins of hell) springs of temptation.

Water was the first drink in the world, and water must be the first drink at the devil's banquet. There is more in it yet : the devil

shews a trick of his wit in this title. Water is a
good creature, and many celestial things are
shadowed by it. It is the element wherein we
were baptized ; and dignified to figure the grace
of the Holy Spirit, Matt. iii. 11. Yet this very
name must be given to sin. Indeed, I know the
same things are often accepted in divers senses
by the language of heaven. Leaven is eftsoons
taken for hypocrisy, as in the Pharisees ; for
atheism, as in the Sadducees ; for profaneness, as
in the Herodians ; and generally for sin, by Paul,
1 Cor. v. 7 ; yet by Christ, for grace. Graces are
called waters ; so here vices : but the attribute
makes the difference. Those are 'living waters,'
these are the 'waters of death.' The devil in this
plays the sophister.

We leave then the prescription of the waters,
and come to the description of their natures :
stolen. It is a word of theft, and implies, besides
the action of stealth, some persons active and
passive in this business : some that do wrong,
and steal ; some that suffer wrong, and are
robbed. Robbery is a sin, literally forbidden
only in one commandment, but by inference in
all. What sin is committed, and some person is
not robbed ? Doth not idolatry rob God of his
worship ? Blasphemy of his honour ? Sabbath
impiety of his reserved time ? Doth not irreverence

rob our betters? Murder rob man of his life? Theft of his goods? False testimony of his good name or right?

Since, then, all sins are waters of stealth, it is an inevitable consequent that every sin robs some; let us examine whom. The parties robbed are God, man, ourselves; and there be divers sins rob either of these. Of every circumstance a little, according to the common liking; for some had rather hear many points than learn one: they would have every word a sentence, and every sentence a sermon; as he that wrote the Paternoster in the compass of a penny. Only I entreat you to observe, that this is a thievish banquet, where is nothing but stolen waters; the guests cannot drink a drop but there is injury done. Accordingly, I will jointly proceed to describe the waters of sin at this feast; and withal, to prove them stolen waters, such as rob either our God, our brethren, or ourselves.

The *first* course of these waters are such sins as more immediately rob God; and here, as it is fit, Atheism leads in the rest, a principal vial of these stolen waters.

Atheism is the highest theft against God, because it would steal from him not *sua, sed se*, his goods, but himself.

The second vial is *Heresy*: a dangerous water,

because it soon tickles the brain, and makes the mind drunk. This sin robs God of his truth.

The third vial of this course is *Sacrilege*: a water like some winding Meander, that runs through our corn-fields, and washeth away the truth, God's part. This sin robs God of his goods: Mal. iii. 8, 'Will a man rob God? Yet ye have robbed me. But ye say, Wherein have we robbed thee? In tithes and offerings.' Hence now there is little difference betwixt serving at the altar and starving at the altar. Ministers have many praisers, few raisers; many benedictors, few benefactors.

Plead not that they are not stolen, because conveyed by the ministers' consent; for the right is originally in God. 'You have robbed me,' saith the Lord. The incumbent consenting is not robbed, God is. They zealously require a learned ministry, when themselves embezzle the rewards of learning : they complain of an ignorant, not of a beggarly clergy. They are content we should stand in the pulpit, so long as they may sit in a tithe-shock ; and seem wonderfully affected with the oraculous voice of their minister, but the creaking noise of a tithe-cart into their own barn is better music. Oh the fearful cry of this sin in the ears of God against this land !

These are the sins that immediately rob God,

fitly called by our whorish sorceress 'stolen waters,' which shall be carried away without account. The *second* sort of stolen waters are those sins which mediately rob God, immediately our brethren, depriving them of some comfort or right which the inviolable law of God hath interested them to; for what the law of God, of nature, of nations, hath made ours, cannot be extorted from us without stealth, and may be, even in most strict terms, called stolen waters.

Here, fitly, *Irreverence* is served in first: a water of stealth that robs man of that right of honour wherewith God hath invested him. Even Abimelech, a king, a Gentile king, reverenced Abraham, Gen. xxi.; even stately Herod, poor John Baptist, Mark vi. Yes, let reverence be given to superiority, if it be built on the basis of worthiness; and to age, if it be 'found in the way of righteousness.' Eminency of place and virtue should concur, that greatness and goodness should dwell together; but the 'conscience of reverence' is fetched from God's precept, not man's dignity, Rom. xiii. 5, and therefore the omission is a robbery. The neglect of honour to whom it belongs is a stolen water.

From this foul nest have fluttered abroad all those clamorous bills, slanderous libels, malicious invectives, seditious pamphlets, whence not only good names have been traduced, but good things abused. Self-conceit blows them up with ventosity ; and if others think not as well of them as they of themselves, straight like porcupines they shoot their quills, or like cuttles vomit out ink to trouble the waters.

Murder usurps the second room : red water that robs a man of his life. The sudden quarrels of our age, or at best inconsiderate fury are produced as arguments of valour, a cross word is ground enough for a challenge. We fall out for feathers ; some lie dead in the channel whiles they stood too much for the wall. Not to pledge a health is cause enough to lose health and life too. Oh, who shall wash our land from these aspersions of blood?

There is not a drop of blood thus spilt upon the earth but swells like an ocean, and nothing can dry it up till it be revenged. The most excellent of God's creatures on earth, the beauty, the extract, the abstract, or abridgement of the world, the glory of the workman, the confluence of all honour that mortality can afford, and, what is above all the rest, the image of the almighty God, with pain born, with expense nurtured, must fall in a moment ; and by whom? One son of Adam by another.

Adultery knows her place : a filthy water, yet

in special account at this feast. It may well be called a stolen water; for it robs man of that comfort which the sacred hand of heaven hath knit to him; unravels the bottom of that joy which God hath wound up for him; suborns a spurious seed to inherit his lands; damps his livelihood, sets paleness on his cheek, and impastures grief in his heart. Woe is to him that is robbed,—I mean the bitter woe of a temporal discontent, which is an inseparable consequent of conjugal affection wronged,—but more woe to the robber, who, besides the corporal strokes of heaven's angry hand in this life, shall feel the fearful addition of an eternal woe in hell: Heb. xiii. 4, 'Whoremongers and adulterers God will judge.'

Thievery needs no more than the name to prove it a 'water of stealth.' This robs man of his goods, those temporal things whereof God hath made him a proprietary: a sin which usurers and moneymongers do bitterly rail at. They that are of no religion yet plead religion hard against thieves; they can lay the law to them that have no conscience themselves; they rob a country, yet think themselves honest men, and would hang a poor petty robber for forty pence.

I do not spare with connivance the junior thieves, because I bring their fathers to the bar first. He that shall with a violent or subtle hand, lion-like or fox-like, take away that which God hath made mine, endangers at once his body to the world's, his soul to heaven's, sword of justice ; and shall pass from a temporal bar to the judgment tribunal of Christ.

Slander is a water in great request ; every guest of the devil is continually sipping of this vial. It robs man of his good name, which is above all riches. It is the part of vile men to vilify others, and to climb up to unmerited praise by the stairs of another's disgrace. This is no new dish at some novelist's table, to make a man's discredit as sauce to their meat ; they will toss you the maligned's reputation, with the rackets of reproach, from one to another, and never bandy it away till they have supped. If they want matter, jealousy is fuel enough ; it is crime enough for a formalist (so they term him), that he is but suspected guilty.

The calumniator is a wretched thief, and robs man of the best thing he hath, if it be a true maxim that the efficacy of the agent is in the apt disposition of the patient ; whiles thou deprivest man of his credit, thou takest from him all power to do good. The slanderer wounds three at one blow : (1) The receiver, in poisoning his heart with an uncharitable conceit. (2) The reputation of the slandered : for a man's name is like a glass, if it be once cracked it is soon broken ; every briar is ready to snatch at the torn garment. (3) The worst blow lights on his own soul ; for the arrow will rebound. The slandered scapes best : 'for God shall bring forth his righteousness as the light,' &c., Ps. xxxvii. 6.

These are those hogs in a garden, which root up the flowers of a man's good parts. But if there were no receiver there would be no thief ; men would not so burden themselves with the coals of contumely, if they had nowhere to unload them.

The last vial of this course is *Flattery*, a water taken out of Narcissus's well ; whereof when great men drink plentifully, they grow mad in their own admiration : and when self-love hath once befooled the brains, the devil himself would not wish the train of consequent sins longer. This is a terrible enchantment, that robs men with delight ; that counts simplicity a silly thing, and will swear a falsehood to please a Felix.

The *third* and last sort of vials served in at this course are stolen waters which immediately rob ourselves. The devil finds us cheer at our own cost ; and with cates stolen from our own possessions, he makes us a bounteous feast. Truth is, every cup of sin we drink of is a water

that, at least indirectly, robs ourselves : neither
can we feed on atheism, heresy, sacrilege, murder,
adultery, but we rifle our souls of grace, our consciences of peace ; for the devil's banquet never
makes a man the fatter for his feeding.   The
guests, the more they eat, the more lean and
meagre they look : their strength goes away with
their repast, as if they fed on nothing but sauce ;
and all their sweet delicates in taste were but
fretting in digestion, like vinegar, olives, or pulse ;
neither doth batten and cherish, because it wants
a blessing unto it.   Only it gets them a stomach :
the more heartily they feed on sin, the greater
appetite they have to it.

The first vial of this nature is *Pride* : a stolen
water indeed, but derived from thine own fountain.
It may strike God, offend thy brother, but it doth
immediately rob thyself.   The decoration of the
body is the devoration of the substance : the back
wears the silver that would do better in the purse.
The grounds are unstocked to make the back
glister.   Adam and Eve had coats of beasts'
skins, Gen. iii. 21 ; but now many beasts, flesh,
skins, and all, will scarce furnish a prodigal
younger son of Adam with a suit.   And as many
sell their tame beasts in the country to enrich
their wild beasts in the city, so you have others
that to revel at a Christmas will ravel out their

patrimonies. Pride and good husbandry are neither kith nor kin. They whose fathers could sit and tell their Michaelmas-hundreds, have brought December on their estates, by wearing May on their backs all the year. Why do ye kill your souls with sins, and garnish your bodies with braveries? The maid is finer than the mistress, which, St Jerome saith, would make a man laugh, a Christian weep to see. Hagar is tricked up, and Sarah put into rags; the soul goes every day in her work-day clothes, unhighted with graces, whiles the body keeps perpetual holiday in gayness.

The next cup of these stolen waters is *Epicurism*: a water which whiles we sup of, we suck ourselves; a sin that whiles men commit it, it commits them, either to the highway or the hedges; and from thence, either by a writ or a warrant, an arrest or a *mittimus*, to the prison.

Perhaps, you will say, they are more kind to themselves; not a whit, for they wrap up death in their full morsels, and swallow it as pills in the pap of delicacy. They overthrow nature with that should preserve it, as the earth that is too rank mars the corn. They make short work with their estates, and not long with their lives; as if they knew that if they lived long, they must be beggars: therefore at once they make haste to

43

spend their livings, and end their lives. Full
suppers, midnight revels, morning junkets, give
them no time to blow, but add new to their
indigested surfeits. They are the devil's crammed
fowls, like Æsop's hens, too fat to lay, to produce
the fruits of any goodness.

The third vial is *Idleness*: a filching water
too, for it steals away our means, both to get
goods and to be good. It is a rust to the
conscience, a thief to the estate. The idle man is
the devil's cushion, whereupon he sits and takes
his ease. He refuseth all works, as either thank-
less or dangerous. Thus charactered, he had
rather freeze than fetch wood; he had rather
steal than work, and yet rather beg than take
pains to steal; and yet in many things rather
want than beg. Saith Melancthon,—sluggards
are thieves; they rob insensibly the commonwealth, most sensibly themselves: 'Poverty comes
on him as an armed man,' Prov. xxiv. 34.

The fourth cup is *Envy*: water of a strange
and uncouth taste. There is no pleasure in being
drunk with this stolen water; for it frets and
gnaws both in palates and entrails. There is no
good relish with it, either in taste or digestion.
The envious man is an incompetent hearer; his
ears are not fit to his head. If he hears good of
another, he frets that it is good; if ill, he is

discontent that he may not judge him for it. If wronged, he cannot stay God's leisure to quit him : he is straight either a Saul or an Esau ; by secret ambushes, or by open hostility, he must carve himself a satisfaction. No plaster will heal his pricked finger, but his heart-blood that did it ; if he might serve himself, he would take unreasonable pennyworths. But malice is ever blind, to see what sequel attends her courses. The envious man is content to lose one eye of his own, so he may put out both his neighbour's ; nay, which is worse, he will lose both his own to put out one of his. The least trespass shall not pass without suit. The devil can send him on a very slight errand to Westminster Hall. Be the case never so broken, if the lawyers' wit can stitch it together, that it may hold to a *nisi prius*, it is enough.

Envy is thrown like a ball of wild-fire at another's barn ; rebounds and fires thine own. The swallow having crossed some lands and seas returns next summer to her old chimney ; the arrow of malice shot far off turns upon his heart that set it flying. Bless yourselves ; you know not whither you will be carried if once you be horsed on the back of the envious man. Forbear, then, this water, as thou lovest thy health, blood, life, and peace.

45

The fifth cup is *Drunkenness* : a vial of the waters of stealth, a liquid food literally taken. For that which ebriety sins withal is wine and strong drink. 'Woe to them that are mighty to devour drink !' Isa. v. 22 ; and strong to carry it away, for their hability encourageth their more frequent sinning. But drunkenness, as it is a cup of this service, is a special water of itself at the devil's banquet. This sin is a horrible self-theft ; God hath passed his word against him : 'The drunkard and the glutton shall come unto poverty, and drowsiness shall clothe a man with rags,' Prov. xxiii. 21. He that drinks more in a day than he can earn in a week, what will his gettings come to at the year's end ? There is no remedy ; he must shake hands with beggary, and welcome it into his company. How many, in the compass of our knowledge, have thus robbed themselves, and been worse enemies to their own estates than the most mischievous thieves ! Thieves cannot steal land, unless they be Westminster Hall thieves, crafty contenders that eat out a true title with a false evidence ; but the drunkard robs himself of his lands. Now he dissolves an acre, and then an acre, into the pot, till he hath ground all his ground at the maltquern, and run all his patrimony through his throat. Thus he makes himself the living tomb of his forefathers, of his posterity. He needs not trouble his sick mind with a will, nor distrust the fidelity of executors. He drowns all his substance at the ale-fat, and though he devours much, is the leaner every way. Drunkenness is a costly sin. It is like gunpowder, many a man is blown up by it. He throws his house so long out at windows, till at last his house throws him out at doors. This is the tippler's progress; from luxury to beggary; from beggary to thievery; from the tavern to Tyburn; from the alehouse to the gallows.

The last vial of these self-stolen waters is *Covetousness*: a dish of drink at this banquet which more come for than for all the rest. The covetous is a cruel thief to himself. He loves money better than his own soul. There is no sin so ugly, so hideous but sent to the covetous man's door in a golden vizor, it shall have entertainment. This sin is like a great beast, which, violently breaking upon God's freehold, makes a gap wide enough for the whole herd to follow. The covetous possesseth the world, and makes use of God; but if a man cannot serve 'God and Mammon,' he can much less serve 'Mammon and God.' God scorns to be set after the world. He heavens himself on earth, and for a little pelf cozens himself of bliss. He steals quiet from his

47

own bones, peace from his conscience, grace from his soul. Is not this a thief?

Many a wretched father plays the thief with himself, and starves his own carcase to leave wealth to his babe. He lives on roots that his prodigal heir may feed on pheasants; he keeps the chimney corner that his heir may frequent ordinaries; he drinks water that his heir may drink wine, and that to drunkenness. Though he be richer than Dives he lives like an alchymist.

Thus the covetous man pines in plenty, like Tantalus, up to the chin in water, yet thirsty. He that hath no power to take part of God's blessings, which he keepeth, plays the thief finely, and robs himself. His extortion hath erst stolen from others, and now he plays rob-thief, and steals from himself. They say the rule of charity should be fetched from home. He that is miserable to himself will never be liberal to others; he that pines himself, God bless me from begging at his door! The niggard's looks to his entering guests are like Diana's image in Chios, which frowned with a lowering countenance on all that came into the temple, but looked blithe and smiled on them that departed. This is he that thinks there are no such angels as his golden ones; no such paradise as in his counting-house. He cares not to run quick to the devil of an errand, so gain sends him, and pays him for his pains. He is a special guest at the devil's board, and never misseth his ordinary, which he affects the more because he pays nothing.

We have now ended the service of the waters with, (1) The prescription of their being, *waters* ; and, (2) The description of their natures, *stolen.*

All stolen things are accountable for ; the law of all nations hath provided that every man may enjoy his own. God is a just judge, a retributor of every man his own. No thief can escape the apprehension of his pursuivants, the appearance to his sessions, the penalty of his sentence. He hath appointed a general assizes, to which there is a necessity of appearance. At which time an account is not avoidable. What then will be the success of these stolen waters?

All must be summoned, their debts summed, their doom sentenced. The impartial conscience from the book of their lives shall give in clear evidence. There is no retaining of counsel, no bribing for a partial censure, no trick of demur, no putting off and suspending the sentence, no evading the doom.

Lo the success of these stolen waters. You hear their nature : time hath prevented their sweetness. God of his mercy, that hath given us

his word to inform our judgment, vouchsafe by
his Spirit to reform our consciences, that we may
conform our lives to his holy precepts! For this
let us pray, &c.

> 'What here is good, to God ascribed be,
> What is infirm belongs of right to me.'

THE FATAL BANQUET

THE BREAKING-UP OF THE FEAST

Stolen waters are sweet, and bread eaten in
secret is pleasant.—Prov. ix. 17.

'STOLEN waters are sweet.' It is the speech of
the 'father of lies,' and therefore to carry little
credit with us. Sweet! to none but those that are
lust-sick; like them that are troubled with the green
sickness, that think chalk, and salt, and rubbish,
savoury. It is a strangely-affected soul that can
find sweetness in sin. Sin is the depravation of
goodness. The same that rottenness is in the apple,
sourness in the wine, putrefaction in the flesh, is
sin in the conscience. Can that be sweet which
is the depraving and depriving of all sweetness?
Let any subtlety of the devil declare this riddle.
The pre-existent privations were deformity, confusion, darkness. The position of their opposite
perfections was the expulsion of those foul
contraries. Sin comes like bleak and squalid
winter, and drives out these fair beauties; turns
the sunshine to blackness, calmness to tempests,
ripeness to corruption, health to sickness, sweetness to bitterness.

They desperately thrust themselves on the pikes of that threatened woe, Isa. v., that dare say of 'bitter, It is sweet'; and consent to the devil in the pleasantness of his cheer, when the impartial conscience knows it is 'gall and wormwood,' Jer. ix. 15. Yet such is the strong enchantment whereby Satan hath wrought on their affections, that bloodiness, lust, perjury, oppression, malice, pride, carry with these guests an opinion of sweetness. If frothy and reeling drunkenness, lean and raking covetousness, meagre and bloodwasted envy, keen and rankling slander, nasty and ill-shapen idleness, smooth and fair-spoken flattery, be comely, what is deformed? If these be sweet, there is no bitterness. But though the devil be not 'an angel of light,' yet he would be like one, 2 Cor. xi. 14. Though he never speaks truth, yet he would often speak the colour of truth, Matt. iv. 6. Therefore, let us observe what fallacies and deceitful arguments he can produce to make good this attribute, and put the probability of sweetness into his stolen waters. For the devil would not be thought a dunce; too weak to hold a position, though it be never so absurd. Stolen waters, iniquities, are sweet to the wicked in three respects: (1) Because they are stolen; (2) Because they are cheap; (3) Because they give delight and persuaded content to the flesh.

(1) Stolen or forbidden. Even in this consists the approbation of their sweetness, that they come by stealth, and are compassed by dangerous and forbidden pains. Theft delights, even in that it is theft. The fruits of a wicked man's own orchard are not so pleasant-tasted as his neighbours'; neither do they reserve their due sweetness if they be freely granted. But as the proverb hath it, apples are sweet when they are plucked in the gardener's absence. Eve liked no apple in the garden so well as the forbidden, Gen. iii. 6. Antiochus scorns venison as base meat if it be not lurched. It is a humour as genuine to our affections as moisture is inseparable to our bloods, that we run mad after restrained objects. We tread those flowers under our disdainful feet, which, mured from us, we would break through stone walls to gather. The liberty of things brings them into contempt; neglect and dust-heaps lie on the accessible stairs. Difficulty is a spur to contention; and there is nothing so base as that which is easy and cheap. The two great lights of heaven, that rule in their courses the day and night, are beholden to no eyes for beholding them so much as when they are eclipsed. We admire things less wonderful, because more rare. If the sun should rise but once in our age, we would turn Persians, and worship it.

Thus we all long for restrained things, and dote on difficulties; but look with an overly scorn and winking neglect on granted faculties. Pharaoh is sick of God's plague; the peaceable dismission of Israel will cure him: he sees his medicine; no, he will be sicker yet, Israel shall not go, Exod. viii. Oh that these who wrestle with God would think that the more fiercely and fierily they assault him, they are sure of the sorer fall! The harder the earthen vessel rusheth upon the brazen, the more it is shivered in pieces. But nothing doth give the ungodly such content as that they dangerously pull out of the jaws of difficulty. No flowers have so good a smell as the stolen; no repast so savoury as the cates of theft.

The second argument of their sweetness is their cheapness. The sins of stealth please the wicked because they are cheap; what a man gets by robbery comes without cost. The ungodly would spare their purse, though they lay out of their conscience. They will favour the temporal estates, though their eternal pay for it. Judas had rather lose his soul than his purse; and for thirty silverlings he sells his Master to the Pharisees, and himself to the devil. Yet when all is done, he might put his gains in his eye. It is but their conceit of the cheapness; they pay dear for it in the upshot. The devil is no such frank chapman, to sell his wares for nothing. He would not proffer Christ the kingdoms without a price ; he must be worshipped for them, Matt. iv. The guests carry not a draught from his table, but they must make courtesy to him for it.

The devil's banquet is not yet done ; there is more cheer a-coming. The water-service is ended. Now begin cates of another nature ; or, if you will, of another form, but the nature is all one : the same method of service, the same manner of junkets. It may be distinguished, as the former, into (1) A prescription, *de quo, bread.* (2) A description, *de quanto, bread of secrecies.* (3) An ascription, *de quali, bread of pleasure.*

Observe how the devil is God's ape, and strives to match and parallel him, both in his words and wonders. He follows him, but with unequal steps. If Christ have his 'waters of life' at the Lamb's wedding-feast, the devil will have his waters too at lust's banquet. If 'the Highest give his thunder, hailstones, and coals of fire,' Ps. xviii. 13 (as to Elias's sacrifice), the red dragon doth the like : Rev. xiii. 13, 'He maketh fire to come down from heaven in the sight of men.' If Moses turn his rod to a serpent, the sorcerers do the like ; but yet they fall short, for Moses's rod devoured all theirs, Exod. vii. 12. Thus, if Christ

at his table offer to his saints his own body for
bread, blood for wine, in a mystical sort; the
devil will proffer some such thing to his guests,
bread and waters, waters of stealth, bread of
secrecy. He is loath to give God the better; he
would not do it in heaven, and therefore was
turned out; and do you think he will yet yield
it? No, in spite of God's water of crystal, Rev.
xxii., peace and glory, he will have his waters of
Acheron, guilt and vanity. But, by Satan's leave,
there is a bread that nourisheth not: Isa. lv. 2,
'Wherefore do ye spend money for that which is
not bread? and your labour for that which
satisfieth not?' It seems, but is not, bread; and,
if it be, yet it satisfies not. This bread the
tempter offers is called secret bread, or the bread
of secrecy, nay, of secrecies; for sin is not like the
rail that sits alone, but like the partridges, who
fly by coveys. *Secret*: this will be found a
fraudulent dimension; for there is nothing so
secret that shall not be made manifest. *God sees.*
There is nothing secret to his eye. He sees our
sins in the book of eternity, before our own hearts
conceived them. He sees them in our hearts
when our inventions have given them form, and
our intentions birth. He sees their action on the
theatre of this earth, quite through the scene of
our lives. He sees them when his wrathful eye

takes notice of them, and his hand is lift up to
punish them. There is nothing so secret and
abstracted from the senses of men, that it may
either lurk from the eye, or escape from the hand
of God. No master of a family is so well acquaint-
ed with every corner of his house, or can so readily
fetch any casket or box he pleaseth, as the Master
of 'the whole family in heaven and earth,' Eph. iii.
15, knows all the angles and vaults of the world.

This forest of man and beast, the world,
grows from evil to worse; like Nebuchadnezzar's
dreamed image, Dan. ii. 32, whose 'head was
golden, silver arms, brazen thighs, but his feet
were of iron and clay.' What Ovid did but
poetize, experience doth moralise, our manners
actually perform. This last stage is (as it must
be) the worst. Sin was wont to love privacy,
as if she walked in fear. The tippler kept his
private ale-bench, not the market-place; the
adulterer his chamber, not (with Absalom, 2 Sam.
xvi. 22) the house-top; the thief was for the night,
or sequestrate ways; the corrupt lawyer took
bribes in his study, not in the open hall; but
now our sins scorn the dark. Men are so far
from being ashamed of their fruitless lives, Rom.
vi. 21, that they commit evil, boast that they
committed, and defend that they boasted. 'Pride
is worn as a chain, and cruelty as a garment,'

Ps. lxxiii. 6; as proud of the fashion. Our consciences take no notice of our own iniquities; but they complain in the audience-court of heaven, and sue out an outlawry against us. So impudent and unblushing is our wickedness, that with the prophet we may complain, 'Were they ashamed when they had committed abomination? nay, they were not at all ashamed; neither could they blush,' Jer. vi. 15, viii. 12 (both places in the same words). Our sins keep not low water, the tide of them is ever swelling; they are objects to the general eye, and proud that they may be observed. And let me tell you, many of the sins I have taxed, as secret and silent as you take them, and as hoarsely as they are thought to speak, are no less than thunder to heaven, and lightning to men. They do vocally ascend, that would actually, if they could.

The labourer's hire cries in the gripolous landlord's hand, James v. 4. The furrows of the encloser cry, complain, nay, weep against him; for so is the Hebrew word, Job xxxi. 38. The vain-glorious builder hath 'the stone crying out of the wall against him, and the beam out of the timber answering it,' Hab. ii. 11. The blasphemer's 'tumult cries, and is come up into the ears of God.' The oppressor's rage and violence reacheth up to heaven, and 'is continually before me, saith the Lord,' Jer. vi. 7. These are crying sins, and

have shrill voices in heaven; neither are they
submiss and whispering on the earth.

To be short: most men are either publicans
or Pharisees,—either they will do no good, or
lose that they do by ostentation. Many act the
part of a religious man, and play devotion on the
world's theatre, that are nothing beside the stage;
all for sight; angels in the highway, devils in the
byway; so monstrous out of the church that they
shame religion.

Take heed, beloved! hell was not made for
nothing. The devil scorns to have his court
empty: you will not bend, you shall break; you
will not serve God, God will serve himself of you.
How many stand here guilty of some of these
sins! How many may say with Æneas, *Et
quorum pars magna fui*, whereof I have a great
share! Many cry out, 'The days are evil,' whiles
they help to make them worse. All censure,
none amend. If every one would pluck a brand
from this fire, the flame would go out of itself.

I would willingly lead you through some
suburbs before I bring you to the main city of
desolation, and shew you the wretched conclusion
of this banquet, and confusion of these guests.
All which arise from the conterminate situation,
or, if I may so speak, from the respondent opposi-
tion of these two sermons, Wisdom's and Folly's,

—that is, God's and Satan's. For this sad sequel
is, if not a relative, yet a redditive demonstration
of their misery; for after the infection of sin
follows that infliction of punishment.

All sinful joys are dammed (if not damned) up
with a *but*. They are troubled with a *but*-plague,
like a bee with a sting in her tail. They have a
worm that crops them, nay, gnaws asunder their
very root; though they shoot up more hastily,
and spread more spaciously than Jonah's gourd.
There is great preparation of this banquet, pro-
peration to it, participation of it; all is carried
with joy and jouisance : there is a corrective *but*
spoils all in the upshot; a little coloquintida, that
embitters the broth; a perilous, a pernicious rock,
that splits the ship in the haven. When all the
prophecies of ill success have been held as
Cassandra's riddles, when all the contrary winds
of afflictions, all the threatened storms of God's
wrath, could not dishearten the sinner's voyage
to these Netherlands, here is a *but* that shipwrecks all; the very mouth of a bottomless pit,
not shallower than hell itself.

It is observable that Solomon's proverbial
says are so many select aphorisms, containing,
for the most part, a pair of cross and thwart
sentences, handled rather by collation than relation, whose conjunction is disjunctive. The

proverbs are not joined with an *et* but an *at*, with
a *but* rather than with an *and*. 'Stolen waters
are sweet,' &c.; '*but* he knoweth not,' &c. It
stands in the midst, like a rudder or oar, to turn
the boat another way. 'Rejoice, O young man,'
&c.; '*but* know that for all these things God will
bring thee to judgment,' &c., Eccles. xi. 9. All
runs smooth, and inclines to the bias of our own
affections, till it lights upon this rub. The Babel
of iniquity is built up apace, till confusion steps
in with a *but*. It is like the sudden clap of a
serjeant on a gallant's shoulder. He is following
his lusts, full scent and full cry; the arrest strikes
him with a *but*, and all is at a loss.

As in a fair summer's morning, when the lark
hath called up the sun, and the sun the husbandman; when the earth hath opened her shop of
perfumes, and a pleasant wind fans coolness
through the air; when every creature is rejoiced
at the heart, on a sudden the furious winds burst
from their prisons, the thunder rends the clouds,
and makes way for the lightning, and the spouts
of heaven stream down showers; a hideous
tempest sooner damps all the former delight than
a man's tongue can well express it. With no less
content do these guests of sin pass their life;
they eat to eat, drink to drink, often to sleep,
always to surfeit; they carol, dance, spend their

present joys, and promise themselves infallible supply. On a sudden this *but* comes like an unlooked-for storm, and turns all into mourning, and such mourning as Rachel had for her children, that will not be comforted, because their joys are not. This is their sad epilogue, or rather the breaking off their scene in the midst. The banquet of stolen waters and secret bread is pleasant; *but* 'the dead are there, and the guests be in the depths of hell.' The devil doth but cozen the wicked with his cates: as before in the promise of delicacy, so here of perpetuity.

He sets the countenance of continuance on them, which indeed are more fallible in their certainty than flourishable in their bravery. Their banqueting-house is very slippery, Ps. lxxiii. 18; and the feast itself a mere dream. You that crown your days with rosebuds, and flatter your hearts with a kingdom over pleasures, think of a low grave for your bodies, and a lower room for your souls. It is the subtlety of our common enemy to conceal this woe from us so long, that we might see it and feel it at once. For if we could but foresee it, we would fear it; if we truly feared it, we would use the means not to feel it.

Solomon's Sermon spends itself upon two circumstances :—

The person tempting, or the harlot, is vice ;

ugly and deformed vice : that with glazed eyes, sulphured cheeks, pied garments, and a Siren's tongue, wins easy respect and admiration. When the heat of tentation shall glow upon concupiscence, the heart quickly melts. The wisest, Solomon, was taken and snared by a woman ; which foul adultery bred as foul an issue, or rather a worse, idolatry. Satan therefore shapes his temptation in the lineaments of a harlot, as most fit and powerful to work upon man's affections. Certain it is that all delighted vice is a spiritual adultery.

The covetous man couples his heart to his gold ; the gallant is incontinent with his pride ; the corrupt officer fornicates with bribery ; the usurer sets continual kisses on the cheek of his security. The heart is set where the hate should be ; and every such sinner spends his spirits to breed and see the issue of his desires. Sin, then, is the devil's harlot, which being tricked up in tempting colours, draws in visitants, giving the kisses of pleasure, and promising them perpetual. A cheat is offered to a tradesman, an enclosure to a landlord, an underhand fee clapped in the left hand of a magistrate ; if they be evil, and corruption hath first marshalled the way, the field is won. They never treat with sin for truce, or pause on an answer, but presently yield the fort of their conscience. No wonder, then, if the devil's harlot be so bold, when she is so sure of welcome. It is our weakness that gives Satan encouragement ; if we did resist, he would desist. Our weak repulses hearten and provoke his fiercer assaults.

Sin deals with her guests as that bloody prince, that having invited many great states to a solemn feast, flattered and singled them one by one, and cut off all their heads. As fatal a success attends on the flatteries of sin. Oh, then, fly this harlot, that carries death about her. Go aloof from her door, as, they say, the devil doth by the cross; but (lest that savour of supposition, nay, of superstition) do thou in sincere devotion fly from sin, as from a serpent. She hath a Siren's voice, mermaid's face, a Helen's beauty to tempt thee ; but a leper's touch, a serpent's sting, a traitorous hand to wound thee. The best way to conquer sin is by Parthian war, to run away.

Thus have we described the temptress. The *tempted* follows, who are here called the *dead*. There be three kinds of death—corporal, spiritual, eternal : corporal, when the body leaves this life ; spiritual, when the soul forsakes and is forsaken of grace ; eternal, when both shall be thrown into hell. The first is the separation of the soul from the body ; the second the separation of body and soul from grace; and the third is the separation of them both from everlasting happiness. Man hath two parts by which he lives, and two places wherein he might live if he obeyed God : earth for a time, heaven for ever. This harlot, sin, deprives either part of man in either place of true life, and subjects him both to the first and second death.

Spiritual death is called the death of the soul; which consisteth not in the loss of her understanding and will, (these she can never lose, no, not in hell,) but of the truth and grace of God, wanting both the light of faith to direct her, and the strength of love to incite her to goodness. 'For to be carnally minded is death; but to be spiritually minded is life and peace,' Rom. viii. 6. The soul is the life of the body, God of the soul. The spirit gone utterly from us, we are dead. And so especially are the guests of Satan dead. 'You hath he quickened, who were dead in trespasses and sins.'

Temptation assaults the heart; consent wounds it : it lies sick of action; it dies by delight in sin; it is buried by custom. The bell hath tolled for it; God's word hath mourned; the church hath prayed for it; but what good can signs and prayers do, when we voluntarily yield our heart to him that violently kills it?

Thus God leaves the heart, and Satan seizeth on it, whose gripes are not gentler than death.

Thus the habit of sin takes away the sense of sin ; and the conscience, that was at first raw and bleeding, as newly wounded, is now 'seared as with a hot iron,' 1 Tim. iv. 2. The conscience of a wicked man first speaks to him, as Peter to Christ, Matt. xvi. 22, 'Master, look to thyself.' But he stops her mouth with a violent hand. Yet she would fain speak to him, like the importunate widow, to do her justice. He cannot well be rid of her, therefore he sets her a day of hearing, and when it is come faileth her. She cries yet louder for audience; and when all his corrupt and bribed affections cannot charm her silence, he drowns her complaints at a tavern, or laughs her out of countenance at a theatre. But if the pulse beats not, the body is most dangerously sick ; if the conscience prick not, there is a dying soul. It is a lawless school where there is an awless monitor. The city is easily surprised where the watch cannot ring the alarms. No marvel if numbness be in the heart when there is dumbness in the conscience.

These are the dead guests ; dead to all goodness. Deaf ears, lame feet, blind eyes, maimed hands, when there is any employment for them in God's service. 'Eyes full of lust,' void of com-

66

passion; ears deaf to the word, open to vanity; feet swift to shed blood, slow to the temple; hands open to extortion, shut to charity. To all religion the heart is a piece of dead flesh. No love, no fear, no care, no pain can penetrate their senseless and remorseless hearts. Through many wounds they come to this death. At first they sin and care not, now they sin and know not. The often taken potion never works. Even the physic of reproof turns now to their hardening. Oh that our times were not full of this deadness!

The third person here inserted is the *attempted*, the new guest whom she strives to bring in to the rest. He is described by his ignorance: 'He knoweth not' what company is in the house, 'that the dead are there.' It is the devil's policy, when he would ransack and rob the house of our conscience, like a thief to put out the candle of our knowledge; that we might neither discern his purposes nor decline his mischiefs. He hath had his instruments in all ages to darken the light of knowledge.

True it is that knowledge without honesty doth more hurt. The unicorn's horn, that in a wise man's hand is helpful, is in the beast's head hurtful. If a man be a beast in his affections, in his manners; the more skilful, the more wilful. Knowledge hath two pillars, learning and discretion. The greatest scholar without his two eyes, of discretion and honesty, is like blind Samson ; apt to no good, able to much mischief. Prudence is a virtue of the soul, nay, the very soul of virtue, the mistress to guide the life in goodness. All moral virtues are beholden to Wisdom. She directs bounty what to give, when to give, where to give ; and fortitude, with whom, for what, and how to fight. Knowledge is excellent to prevent dangers imminent, and to keep us from the snares of this ' strange woman.' But if the devil in our days should have no guests but those that are merely ignorant, his rooms would be more empty than they are, and his ordinary break for want of customers. But now-a-days,—alas ! when was it much better, and yet how can it be much worse? —we know sin, yet affect it, act it. Time was, we were ignorant and blind ; now we have eyes and abuse them. Tyre and Sidon burn in hell, and their smoke ascends for evermore, that had no preaching in their cities ; but our country is sown with mercies, and ourselves fatted with the doctrine of life. Who shall excuse our lame, lean, and ill-favoured lives? Let us beware Bethsaida's woe. If the heathen shall wring their hands for their ignorance, then many Christians shall rend their hearts for their disobedience.

THE FATAL BANQUET

Such is Satan's banqueting house, and such the guests—the dead are there!

But when Heaven is the house and God the host how changed the scene! In thy presence is fulness of joy; and at thy right hand are pleasures for evermore. He that walketh righteously, he shall dwell on high; his place of defence shall be the munitions of rocks: bread shall be given him; his waters sure. His joys are certain and stable; no alteration, no alternation shall impair them. These four things concur that make a perfect feast. A good time, eternity; a good place, heaven; a good company, the saints; good cheer, glory.

God himself is the feast-maker: he is landlord of the world, and 'filleth every living thing with goodness.' The king favoureth all his subjects, but they of his court stand in his presence, and partake of his princely graces. God's bounty extends to the wicked also, but the saints shall only sit at his table in heaven.

The cheer is beyond all sense, all science: 1 Cor. ii. 9, 'Eye hath not seen, nor ear heard, neither have entered into the heart of man, the things God hath prepared for them that love him.' The eye sees much, the ear hears more, the heart conceives most; yet all short of apprehension, much more of comprehension, of these pleasures.

69

Therefore 'enter thou into thy Master's joy,' for it is too great to enter into thee.

The company is excellent : the glorious presence of the blessed Trinity—the Father that made us, the Son that bought us, the Holy Ghost that brought us to this place ; the holy and unspotted angels, that rejoiced at our conversion on earth, much more at our consolation in heaven ; all the patriarchs, prophets, saints, before the law, in the law, in the gospel ; the full communion of saints. Here, the more the merrier, yea, and the better cheer too. Oh the sweet melody of hallelujahs, which so many glorified voices shall sing to God in heaven ! the hoarseness of sin and the harshness of punishment being separated from us with a bill of everlasting divorce.

Admirable is the banqueting-place : the high court of heaven, where our apparel shall be such as beseemeth the attendants on the King of kings, even 'the fashion of the glorious body of Christ,' Phil. iii. 21. Take here a slight relish of the cheer in God's kingdom, where your welcome shall be answerable to all the rest : 'Eat, O my friends ; and make you merry, O well-beloved,' Cant. v. 1. And then, as those that have tasted some delicate dish find other plain meats but unpleasant, so you that have tasted of heavenly things cannot but contemn the best worldly

pleasures.   And therefore as some dainty guest,
knowing there is so pleasant fare to come, let us
reserve our appetites for that, and not suffer
ourselves to be cloyed with the coarse diet of the
world.   Thus as we fast on the eves that we may
feast on the holidays, let us be sure that, after our
abstinence from the surfeits of sin, we shall be
everlastingly fed and fatted with the mercies of
God.   Which resolution the Lord grant us here;
which banquet the Lord give us hereafter!   Amen.

GOD'S BOUNTY;

OR,

THE BLESSINGS OF BOTH HIS HANDS

Length of days is in her right hand; and in her left hand riches and honour.—Prov. iii. 16.

By Wisdom here we understand the Son of God, the Saviour of man. In the first to the Corinthians, chap. i. 24, he is called the 'wisdom of God.' Col. ii. 3, 'In him are hid all the treasures of wisdom and knowledge.'

Wisdom is formerly commended for her beauty, here for her bounty: 'Length of days is in her right hand; in her left, riches and honour.' Conceive her a glorious queen sitting on a throne of majesty, and calling her children about her, to the participation of those riches which from everlasting she had decreed them.

Not to travel far for distribution, the parts of this text are as easily distinguished as the right hand from the left. Here be two hands, and they contain two sorts of treasures. The *right* hand

72

hath in it 'length of days'; the *left*, 'riches and honour.'

The right hand is, upon good reason, preferred, both for its own worth whereby it excels, and for the worth of the treasure which it contains. It hath ever had the dignity, as the dexterity.

Length of days is the treasure it holds. This cannot be properly understood of this mortal life, though the sense may also stand good with such an interpretation. 'For by me,' saith Wisdom, 'thy days shall be multiplied, and the years of thy life shall be increased,' Prov. ix. 11. Wisdom is the mother of abstinence, and abstinence the nurse of health; whereas voluptuousness and intemperance, as the French proverb hath it, digs its own grave with the teeth.

There is nothing made perfectly happy but by eternity; as nothing but eternity can make perfect misery. Were thy life a continued scene of pleasures, on whose stage grief durst never set his unwelcome foot; were the spoil of Noah's ark the cates of thy table; hadst thou King Solomon's wardrobe and treasury; did the West Indies send thee all her gold, and the East her spices; and all these lying by thee whiles a late succession of years without cares snows white upon thy head; thou wert ever indulgent to thyself, and health to thee;—yet suddenly there comes an unpartial pursuivant, Death, and he hath a charge to take thee away bathing thyself in thy delights. Alas! what is all thy glory but a short play, full of mirth till the last act, and that goes off in a tragedy? Couldest thou not have made Death more welcome if he had found thee lying on a pad of straw, feeding on crusts and water-gruel? Is not thy pain the more troublesome because thou wast well? Doth not the end of these temporary joys afflict thee more than if they had never been? Only then eternity can give perfection to pleasure; which because this world cannot afford, let us reckon of it as it is, a mere thoroughfare, and desire our home, where we shall be happy for ever.

In her left hand, riches and honour.—The gift of the *right* hand is large and eternal; of the *left*, short and temporal. Riches and honour are God's gifts, therefore in themselves not evil. Saith Augustine—that they may not be thought evil, they are given to good men; that they may not be thought the best good, they are given also to evil men. A rich man may be a good man, and a poor man may be wicked. Not seldom a russet coat shrouds as high a heart as a silken garment. You shall have a paltry cottage send up more black smoke than a goodly manor. It is not wealth thereof, but vice, that excludes men out of heaven.

74

GOD'S BOUNTY

The friars and Jesuits have very strongly and strangely backbited riches ; but all their railing on it is but behind the back : secretly and in their hearts they love it. When they are out of the reach of eyes, then gold is their sun by day, and silver their moon by night. Some of them for enforced want, like the fox, dispraise the grapes they cannot reach. Or, as Eusebius notes of Licinius the emperor, that he used to rail at learning, and to say nothing worse became a prince, because himself was illiterate ; so they commend nothing more than poverty, because they are, and must be, poor against their wills.

Others of them find fault with riches, whereof they have great store, but would that none should covet it beside themselves. So the cozening epicure made all his fellow-guests believe that the banquet was poisoned, that, all they refusing, he might glut himself alone. These often cheat themselves, and work their own bane : whiles they so beat off others from the world, and wrap themselves up in it to their confusion. The fox in the fable, with divers other beasts, found a rich booty of costly robes and jewels. He persuades the lion that he needs not trouble himself with them, because he is king, and may command all at his pleasure. He tells the stag, that if he should put them on, they would so molest him that he could not escape the huntsmen. For the boar, he says they would evil-favouredly become him; and the wolf he shuffles off with the false news of a fold of lambs hard by, which would do him more good. So all gone, he begins to put on the robes himself, and to rejoice in his lucky fraud. But instantly came the owners, and surprised him, who had so puzzled himself in these habiliments, that he could not by flight escape; so they took him, and hanged him up.

The subtle foxes, Jesuits and friars, dissuade kings from coveting wealth, because of their power to command all; and great men, because it will make them envied and hunted after for their trappings; countrymen it will not become, they say; and all the rest, that it will hinder their journey to heaven. So in conclusion they drive all away, and get the whole world for their master Pope and themselves. But at last these foxes are caught in their own noose; for the devil finds them so wrapped and hampered in these ornaments, and their hearts so besotted on money and riches, that he carries them with as much ease to hell as the chariot drew Pharaoh into the Red Sea.

For us, beloved, we teach you not to cast away the bag, but covetousness. We bid you 'use the world,' but enjoy the Lord. And if you have wealth, 'make you friends with your riches, that they'—so made friends by your charity—'may receive,' and make way for, 'you into ever-lasting habitations,' Luke xvi. 9. It is not your riches of this world, but your riches of grace, that shall do your souls good. 'Not my wealth, nor my blood, but my Christianity makes me noble,' quoth that noble martyr Romanus. And though the philosopher merrily, when he was asked whether were better, wisdom or riches, answered, Riches ; for I have often, said he, seen poor wise men at rich fools' doors, but never rich fools at poor wise men's doors : yet wealth may be joined with wisdom, goodness with greatness. Mary and Martha may be sisters : righteousness and riches may dwell together. Riches are not unrighteous, but to the unrighteous. It is not a sin to have them, but to trust them.

It is easy for that man to be rich that will make his conscience poor. He that will defraud, forswear, bribe, oppress, serve the time, use, abuse all men, all things, swallow any wicked-ness, cannot escape riches. Whereas he whose conscience will not admit of advancing or advan-taging himself by indirect means, sits down with contented poverty. But a good man seldom becomes rich on the sudden. Wealth comes not easily, not quickly, to the honest door. Neither let us envy the gravel that sticks in the throat of injustice. For he that will swallow the bait which hangs on the line of another man's estate, shall be choked with it. Of riches let us never desire more than an honest man may well bear away. I had rather be a miserable saint than a prosperous sinner. When the raising of thy roof is the rasing of another's foundation, 'the stone shall cry out of the wall, and the beam out of the timber shall answer it,' Hab. ii. 11. 'Woe to him that coveteth an evil covetousness to his house!' We think the oppressor's avarice evil only to the houses of the oppressed; but God saith it is most evil to his own. Whether fraud or force bring in unjust gain, it is as a coal of fire put in the thatch of his house.

And to shew that God is not the giver of this, he pours a curse upon it; that often they who thus desire most wealth shall not have it: the world being to them like a froward woman, the more wooed, the further off. Isa. xxxiii. 1, 'Woe to thee that spoilest, and wast not spoiled! when thou shalt cease to spoil thou shalt be spoiled.' Philip was wont to say that an ass laden with gold would enter the gates of any city; but the golden load of bribes and extortions shall bar a man out of the city of God. All that is so gotten is like quicksilver, it will be running. If the

father leave all to his son, yet the son will leave
nothing for his son, perhaps nothing for himself ;
never resting until he hath spread abroad all with
a fork which his father got together with a rake.
We have seen huge hills of wealth, like mountains
of ice, thus suddenly thawed as wax, with the heat
of luxury.   Their wealth is not God's, therefore
he taketh no charge of it.   But the riches of the
good is the riches of God and he will prosper it.

Riches are well disposed or used when piety,
not lust, rules them.   He whom God's blessing
hath made rich gives God his part.   It is reason
that he who gives all should have part of all.
What can then be pleaded for our accursed impropriations?   Did the heavenly Wisdom ever
give you those riches?   Shew us your patent, and
we will believe you.   If ever God did convey his
own portion to you, shew his hand and seal for it.
Where did ever Jesus pass away his royal pre-
rogative, or acknowledge any fine before a judge,
that you say, These are ours?   What money
did you ever pay him for them?   Where is your
acquittance?   Shew your discharge.   Oh, but
you plead prescription !   If you were not past
shame, you would never dare to prescribe against
the eternal God.   *Nullum tempus occurrit regi*,—
The king of heaven had these from the beginning,
and will you now plead prescription?   You may

thus undo the poor minister in these terrene courts, but your plea shall be damned in the courts of God. We can produce his act and deed whereby he separated tenths to himself; have you nothing to shew, and will you take away his inheritance? Go to, you have a law, and by your own law this proceeding is intolerable. You say you hold them by your law, by your law you shall be condemned.

Perhaps you think to make amends for all, for you will increase the stipend of the vicar. When the father hath gotten thousands by the sacrilegious impropriation, the son perhaps may give him a cow's grass, or a matter of forty shillings *per annum;* or bestow a little whiting on the church, and a wainscot seat for his own worship. Yea, more; he may chance to found a little almshouse, and give twelve pence a-piece a-week to six poor people. Oh, this oppressor must needs go to heaven! what shall hinder him? But it will be, as the byword is, in a wheelbarrow: the fiends, and not the angels, will take hold on him.

For is it not a great piece of charity to get five hundred pounds a-year from God, and to bestow twenty marks a-year on the poor? When David, providing for the temple's building, saw how bountifully the princes and people offered, he gives solemn thanks to God, acknowledging that

they had all received this first from him. 1 Chron.
xxix. 14, 'For all things come of thee, and of
thine own have we given thee.' The original is,
'of thine hand.' What here the left hand of God
gave to them, their right hand returns to God.
They did not, as our church-sackers and ran-
sackers do, rob God with the right hand, and
give him a little back with the left; take from
him a pound, and restore him a penny. Well,
you would know whether God hath given you
your wealth; and he says, whatsoever you have
gotten by tenths was none of his giving; and,
besides everlasting malediction, it shall make
your posterity beggars.

The second rule of using our riches well is,
when God hath his own, in the next place, to
render every man his due. If they be God's gifts,
they must be disposed with justice. This is
double—commutative and distributive justice.
The one arithmetical, the other geometrical.
Arithmetical is to give every one alike; geometrical is to give every one according to his
deserts. 'Owe no man anything, but to love one
another.' Indeed there must be some owing, as
there must be some lending; without this mutual
commerce we are worse than savages. But we
must pay again: 'The wicked borroweth and
payeth not again.' Debt is not deadly sin when

A.   81   6

a man hath no means, but when he hath no meaning to pay.

What shall we then say of their goods that break, and defraud others? Come they from God's hand or from the devil's? Surely Satan's right hand gave them, not God's left. Oh that men would see this damnable sin! Methinks their terrified conscience should fear that the bread they eat should choke them; for it is stolen, and stolen bread fills the belly with gravel. They should fear the drink they swallow should poison them; being the very blood of good householders, mixed with the tears of widows and orphans. The poor creditor is often undone, and glad of bread and water; whiles they, like hogs lurking in their sties, fat and lard their ribs with the fruit of others' labours. They rob the husband of his inheritance, the wife of her dowry, the children of their portions; the curse of whole families is against them.

And if this sin lie upon a great man's soul, he shall find it the heavier, to sink him lower into perdition. They are the lords of great lands, yet live upon other men's moneys; they must riot and revel, let the poor commoners pay for it. They have protections; their bodies shall not be molested, and their lands are exempted. What then? Shall they escape? No, their souls shall pay for it. When the poor creditor comes to demand his own, they rail at him, they send him laden away, but with ill words, not good money. In the country they set labourers on work, but they give them no hire. Tut, they are tenants, vassals. Must they therefore have no pay? Yet those very landlords will bate them nothing of their rents. But the riches so had are not of God's giving, but of the devil's lending, and he will make them repay it a thousand-fold in hell.

And here we may fitly proceed to the condemnation of bribery. Deut. xvi. 19, 'A gift blindeth the eyes of the wise.' They that see furthest into the law, and most clearly discern the causes of justice, if they suffer the dusts of bribes to be thrown into their sight, their eyes will water and twinkle, and fall at last to blind connivance. It is a wretched thing when justice is made a hackney that may be backed for money, and put on with golden spurs, even to the desired journey's end of injury and iniquity.

And this is sinful in a justicer though he pass true judgment on the cause; but much more accursed when for this he will condemn the cause he should allow, or allow the cause he should condemn. 'To justify the wicked and condemn the innocent' are alike abomination to the Lord. Far be from our souls this wickedness, that the ear which should be open to complaints is thus stopped with the ear-wax of partiality. Alas, poor Truth, that she must now be put to the charges of a golden ear-pick, or she cannot be heard !

But to shew that these riches are not of God's giving, his anger is hot against them : Job xv. 34, ' Fire shall consume the tabernacles of bribery.' The houses, or tabernacles, the chambers, halls, offices, studies, benches, a fire shall consume them. They may stand for a while, but the indignation of the Lord is kindled ; and if it once begin to burn, all the waters in the south are not able to quench it. These riches, then, come not of God's blessing ; but I pray that God's blessing may be yours, though you want those riches. The Lord send us the gifts of his left hand at his own good pleasure, but never deny us the blessings of his right, for Jesus Christ's sake.

Thus you see this second general point amplified, riches be God's blessings, (not only in themselves, so they are always good, but to us,) when they are gotten honestly, disposed justly, lost patiently. As much happily might be said, *secondly*, for honour, wherein I will briefly consider how and when it is of God.

It is a hard question wherein honour consists. Is it in blood, descending from the veins of noble

ancestors? Not so, except nature could produce
to noble parents noble children. It was a
monstrous tale that Nicippus's ewe should yean
a lion. Though it be true among irrational
creatures, that they ever bring forth their like,
—eagles hatch eagles, and doves doves,—yet in
man's progeny there is often found not so like a
proportion as unlike a disposition. The earthy
part only follows the seed, not that whose form
and attending qualities are from above. Honour
must therefore as well plead a charter of suc-
cessive virtue as of continued scutcheons, or it
cannot consist in blood. The best things can
never be traduced in propagation : thou mayest
leave thy son heir to thy lands in thy will, to thy
honour in his blood ; thou canst never bequeath
him thy virtues. The best qualities do so cleave
to their subjects, that they disdain communication
to others.

That is then only true honour where dignity
and desert, blood and virtue meet together ; the
greatness whereof is from blood, the goodness
from virtue. Among fools dignity is enough without desert ; among wise men desert without
dignity. If they must be separated, desert is
infinitely better. Greatness without virtue is
commended by others' tongues, condemned in
thy own heart. Virtue, though without promotion,

is more comforted in thy own content than disheartened by others' contempt. It is a happy composition when they are united : think it your honour, ye great men, that you are ennobled with virtues; not that you have, but that you deserve honour. Let this that hath been spoken teach us some lessons concerning honour.

If thou have honour, keep it, but trust it not. Nothing is more inconstant; for it depends upon inconstancy itself, the vulgar breath, which is a beast of many heads, and as many tongues, which never keep long in one tune. As they never agree one with another, so seldom do they agree long with themselves. Acts xiv., Paul and Barnabas come to Lystra, and raise an impotent cripple ; hereat the amazed people would needs make them gods, and draw bulls and garlands to the altars for sacrifice to them. Not long after they draw Paul out of the city and stone him. They suddenly turn him from a god to a malefactor, and are ready to kill him, instead of killing sacrifiee to him. Oh the fickleness of that thing which is committed to the keeping of vulgar hands ! Trust not then popularity with thy honour, so it is mutable ; but trust virtue with it, so it is durable. Nothing can make sure a good memory but a good life. It is a foolish dream to hope for immortality and a long-lasting name by a monument of brass or stone. It is not dead stones, but living men, that can redeem thy good remembrance from oblivion. A sumptuous tomb covers thy putrified carcase; and be thy life never so lewd, a commending epitaph shadows all: but the passenger that knew thee tells his friends that these outsides are hypocritical, for thy life was as rotten as is thy corpse; and so is occasioned by thy presumed glory to lay open thy deserved infamy. Neither can the common people preserve thy honour whilst thou livest, nor can these dull and senseless monuments keep it when thou art dead. Only thy noble and Christian life makes every man's heart thy tomb, and turns every tongue into a pen to write thy deathless epitaph.

Lastly, observe that though riches and honour be God's gift, yet they are but the gifts of his left hand: therefore it necessarily follows, that every wise man will first seek the blessings of the right. Godliness is the best riches, riches the worst. Let us strive for the former without condition; for the other, if they fall in our way, let us stoop to take them up. If not let us never covet them.

Here is the main difference between the gifts of God's right hand and of his left. He gives real blessings with the left, but he doth not settle them upon us; he promiseth no perpetuity. But with the graces of his right he gives assurance of everlastingness. Christ calls riches the 'riches of deceitfulness,' Matt. xiii. 22; but grace 'the better part, that shall never be taken away,' Luke x. 42. David compares the wealthy to a flourishing tree that is soon withered, Ps. xxxvii. 35; but faith stablisheth a man like 'Mount Sion, never to be removed,' Ps. cxxv. 1. He that thinks he sits surest in his seat of riches, 'let him take heed lest he fall.' When a great man boasted of his abundance, saith Paulus Emilius, one of his friends told him, that the anger of God could not long forbear so great prosperity. How many rich merchants have suddenly lost all! How many noblemen sold all! How many wealthy heirs spent all! Few Sundays pass over our heads without collections for shipwrecks, fires, and other casualties; demonstrative proofs that prosperity is inconstant, riches casual. And for honour, we read that Belisarius, an honourable peer of the empire, was forced in his old age to beg from door to door: *Obolum date Belisario.* Frederic, a great emperor, was so low brought, that he sued to be made but the sexton of a church.

Oh, then, let us not adhere to these left-hand blessings, but first seek length of days, eternal joys never to be lost. A man may enjoy the other without fault: the sin consisteth either in preferring riches or in comparing them with faith and a good conscience. When God hath assured to a Christian spirit the inheritance of heaven, he joyfully pilgrims it through this world : if wealth and worship salute him by the way, he refuseth not their company ; but they shall not stray him out of his path, nor transport his affections, for his heart is where his hope is, his love is where his Lord is ; even with Jesus his Redeemer, at the right hand of God.

POLITIC HUNTING

*Esau was a cunning hunter, and a man of the
field; and Jacob was a plain man, dwelling
in tents.*—Gen. xxv. 27.

You hear Esau's name; listen to his nature.
God's Spirit gives him this character: 'He was
a cunning hunter.' A name doth not constitute
a nature; yet in Holy Writ very often the nature
did fulfil the name, and answer it in a future
congruence.

The first mark of his character is, 'a cunning
hunter,' wherein we have expressed his *power* and
his *policy*, his strength and his sleight, his brawn
and his brain; his might, he was a hunter; his
wit, he was a cunning hunter.

His Strength: A Hunter.—Hunting in
itself is a delight lawful and laudable, and may
well be argued for from the disposition that God
hath put into creatures. He hath naturally in-
clined one kind of beasts to pursue another for
man's profit and pleasure. He hath given the
dog a secret instinct to follow the hare, the hart,

90

the fox, the boar, as if he would direct a man by the finger of nature to exercise those qualities which his divine wisdom created in them.

There is no creature but may teach a good soul one step towards his Creator. The world is a glass, wherein we may contemplate the eternal power and majesty of God. 'For the invisible things of him from the creation of the world are clearly seen, being understood by the things that are made, even his eternal power and Godhead,' Rom. i. 20. It is that great book of so large a character that a man may run and read it ; yea, even the simplest man, that cannot read, may yet spell out of this book that there is a God. Every shepherd hath this calendar, every ploughman this A B C. What that French poet divinely sung is thus as sweetly Englished—

'The world's a school, where, in a general story,
   God always reads dumb lectures of his glory.'

HIS POLICY : A CUNNING HUNTER.—But we have hunted too long with Esau's strength, let us learn his sleight : 'a cunning hunter.' Hunting requires *tantum artis, quantum martis.* Plain force is not enough, there must be an accession of fraud. There is that common sense in the creatures to avoid their pursuers. Fishes will not be taken with an empty hook ; nor birds with

a bare pipe, though it go sweetly ; nor beasts
with Briareus's strength only, though he had a
hundred hands. Fishes must have a bait, birds
a net, and he that takes beasts must be a cunning
hunter. 'Can a bird fall into a snare upon the
earth where no gin is for him?' Amos iii. 5.
Nay, often both vises and devices, toils and
toilings, strength and stratagems, are all too
little.

A CUNNING HUNTER.—As cunning as he
was to take beasts, he had little cunning to save
himself. How foolish was he to part with his
birthright for a mess of lentil pottage ! His folly
is seen in his slavery to intemperate desires.

It is impossible that a ravenous throat should
lie near a sober brain. There may be in such a
man understanding and reason ; but he neither
hears that nor follows this. A city may have
good laws, though none of them be kept. But as
in sleepers and madmen there is *habitus rationis,
non usus et actus,*—such men have reason, but
want the active use—the belly hath no ears.
Though you would write such men's epitaphs
while they are living, yet you cannot ; for they
have ante-acted their death, and buried themselves alive ; as the French proverb says, They
have digged their grave with their teeth. The

philosopher passing through Vacia the epicure's grounds, said not, Here he lives, but, Here he lies ; as it were dead and sepulchred. The parsimony of ancient times hath been admirable. The Arcadians lived on acorns ; the Argives on apples ; the Athenians on figs ; the Tyrinthians on pears ; the Indians on canes ; the Carmanes on palms ; the Sauromatians on millet ; the Persians, *nasturtio*, with cresses ; and Jacob here made dainty of lentils.

That a man may epicurise on coarse fare ; for lentil pottage was no extraordinary fine diet. But as a man may be a Crassus in his purse, yet no Cassius in his pots ; so, on the contrary, another may be, as it is said of Job, poor to a proverb, yet be withal as voluptuous as Esau. Thus the poor may sin as much in their throat as the rich, and be epicures *tam latè*, though not *tam lautè*,—in as immoderate, though not so dainty fare. Indeed, labour in many bodies requires a more plentiful repast than in others ; and the sedentary gentleman needs not so much meat as his drudging hind. But in both this rule should be observed. Not what will please the throat, but what will content nature ; to eat what a man should, not what he would. The poor man that loves delicate cheer shall not be wealthy ; and the rich man that loves it shall

not be healthy. As cunning as Esau was, here
is one instance of his folly, an intemperate
appetite.

His folly may be argued from his base
estimation of the birthright; that he would so
lightly part from it, and on so easy conditions as
pottage. It seems he did measure it only by the
pleasures and commodities of this life which were
afforded him by it: ver. 32, 'I am ready to die:
and what profit shall this birthright do to me?'
Which words import a limitation of it to this
present world, as if it could do him no good
afterwards; whereupon the Hebrews gather that
he denied the resurrection. In all these circumstances it appeareth, that though Esau was subtle
to take beasts, he had no cunning to hunt out his
own salvation. The wisest for this world are
commonly fools for celestial blessings. They
are wise to do evil; but to do good they have
no knowledge. Let them war, they have their
stratagems; let them plot in peace, they have
their policies. For hunting they have nets; for
fowling, gins; for fishing, baits; not so much as
even in husbandry, but the professors have their
reaches; they know which way the market goes,
which way it will go. Your tradesmen have their
mysteries—they have a stock of good words to
put off a stock of bad wares; in their particular

94

qualities they are able to school Machiavel. But draw them from their centre, earth, and out of their circumference, worldly policies, and you have not more simple fools.

Thus we have taken the first branch of Esau's character: 'he was a cunning hunter.' There is another colour added: 'he was a man of the field'; not a husbandman, but as the Septuagint calls him, a field-man; there was his sport, there was his heart. Some would read it thus, 'because venison was in his mouth,' and so turn his hunting into a metaphor: as if by insinuation he had wound himself into the favour of Isaac. By the way, we may give a reprehension to such mouth-hunters.

If you would know who they are, they are the flatterers, of whom we may say, as huntsmen of their dogs, they are well-mouthed; or rather, ill-mouthed. For an ordinary dog's biting doth not rankle so sore as their licking. Of all dogs they are best likened to spaniels, but that they have a more venomous tongue. They will fawn, and fleer, and leap up, and kiss their master's hand: but all this while they do but hunt him; and if they can spring him once, you shall hear them quest instantly, and either present him to the falcon, or worry and prey on him themselves, perhaps not so much for his flesh as for his feathers. For they love not *dominos*, but *domi-*

95

norum; not their master's good, but their master's goods.

The golden ass, got into sumptuous trappings, thinks he hath as many friends as he hath beasts coming about him. One commends his snout for fairer than the lion's ; another his skin for richer than the leopard's ; another his foot for swifter than the hart's ; a fourth his teeth for whiter and more precious than the elephant's ; a last, his breath for sweeter than the civet beast's. And it is wonder if some do not make him believe he hath horns, and those stronger than bulls', and more virtual than the unicorn's. All this while they do but hunt him for his trappings ; uncase him, and you shall have them baffle and kick him. This doth Solomon insinuate, Prov. xix. 4, ' Riches gather many friends : but the poor is separated from his neighbours.' He says not the rich man, but riches. It is the money, not the man, they hunt.

The great one bristles up himself, and conceits himself higher by the head than all the rest, and is proud of many friends. Alas ! these dogs do but hunt the bird of paradise for his feathers. These wasps do but hover about the gallipot because there is honey in it. The proud fly, sitting upon the chariot-wheel, which, hurried with violence, huffed up the sand, gave out that it was she which made all that glorious dust. The ass, carrying the Egyptian goddess, swelled with an opinion that all those crouches, cringes, and obeisances were made to him. But it is the case, not the carcase, they gape for. So may the chased stag boast how many hounds he hath attending him. They attend indeed, as ravens a dying beast. Actæon found the kind truth of their attendance. They run away as spiders from a decaying house; or as the cuckoo, they sing a scurvy note for a month in summer, and are gone in June or July; sure enough before the fall. These hunters are gone; let them go: for they have brought me a little from the strictness and directness of my intended speech. But as a physician coming to cure doth sometimes receive some of his patient's infection, so I have been led to hunt a little wide, to find out these cunning hunters.

They grew up together, and presently Esau was 'a cunning hunter,' Jacob 'a plain man.' We see that even youth doth insinuate to an observer the inclination and future course of a man. The sprig shooting out of the tree bends that way it will ever grow. 'Teach a child a trade in his youth, and when he is old he will not forget it,' saith Solomon. Esau entered quickly into the black way, which leads to the black gates, that stand ever ready open for black souls. As if he should want rather time for his sport than sport for his time, he begins early, at the very threshold of his life and morning of his years ; his wickedness got the start of his age.

And did he ever stay his course? That foolish parents should be so indulgent to their children's licentiousness! nay, even ready to snib and check their forwardness to heaven with that curb, 'A young saint, an old devil,' and, 'Wild youth is blessed with a staid age!' But indeed, most likely, a young saint proves an old angel, and a young Esau an old devil.

And hence follows the ruin of so many great houses, that the young master is suffered to live like an Esau till he hath hunted away his patrimony, which scarce lasts the son so many years as the father that got it had letters in his name. But what cares he for the birthright? When all is gone, he, like Esau, can live by the sword. He will fetch gold from the Indies but he will have it. But he might have saved that journey, and kept what he had at home. If the usurer hath bought it, though for porridge, he will not part with it again, though they weep tears. It is better to want superfluous means than necessary moderation, especially when the huge Colosses have not sound feet. Vast desires, no less than buildings, where foundations are not firm, sink by their own magnitude. And there comes often fire out of the bramble, Judg. ix. 20, that burns up the men of Shechem, and sets on fire the eagle's nest in the cedars.

Thus literally; let us now come to some moral application to ourselves.

Hunting is, for the most part, taken in the Holy Scripture in the worst sense. So, Gen. x. 9, Nimrod was a hunter, even to a proverb; and that 'before the Lord,' as without fear of his majesty. Now, if it were so hateful to hunt beasts, what is it to hunt men? The wicked oppressors of the world are here typed and taxed, who employ both arm and brain to hunt the poor out of their habitations, and to drink the blood of the oppressed. The commonalty, that by great labour have gotten a little stay for themselves, these they hunt and lay along, and prey upon their prostrate fortunes.

If they be tenants, woe is them: fines, rents, carriages, slaveries, shall drink up the sweat of their brows. There is law against coiners; and it is made treason, justly, to stamp the king's figure in forbidden metals. But what is metal to a man, the image of God! And we have those that coin money on the poor's skins: traitors they are to the King of kings.

The whole country shall feel their hunting.

They hunt commons into severals, tilled grounds
into pastures, that the gleaning is taken from the
poor, which God commanded to be left them, and
all succour, except they can graze in the high-
ways. And to others, to whom their rage cannot
extend, their craft shall ; for they will hoist them
in the subsidies, or overcharge them for the wars,
or vex them with quarrels in law, or perhaps their
servants shall in direct terms beat them. Naboth
shall hardly keep his vineyard, if any nook of it
disfigures Ahab's lordship. If they cannot buy it
on their own price, they will to law for it ; wherein they respect no more than to have a colourable
occasion of contention ; for they will so weary
him, that at last he shall be forced to sell it. But
Tully says of that sale, It is an extorting, not a
purchasing.

Thus the poor man is the beast they hunt ;
who must rise early, rest late, eat the bread of
sorrow, sit with many a hungry meal, perhaps his
children crying for food, while all the fruit of his
pains is served into Nimrod's table. Complain
of this whiles you will, yet, as the orator said of
Verres, *pecuniosus nescit damnari*. Indeed, a
money-man may not be damnified, but he may
be damned. For this is a crying sin, and the
wakened ears of the Lord will hear it, neither
shall his provoked hands forbear it.

POLITIC HUNTING

If I should intend to discover these hunters' plots, and to deal punctually with them, I should afford you more matter than you would afford me time. But I limit myself, and answer all their pleas with Augustine : Their tricks may hold in the common-pleas of earth, not before the king's bench in heaven.

Neither do these cunning hunters forage only the forest of the world, but they have ventured to enter the pale of the church, and hunt there. They will go near to empark it to themselves, and thrust God out. So many have done in this land ; and though it be danger for the poor hare to preach to lions and foxes, I am not afraid to tell them that they hunt where they have nothing to do. Poor ministers are dear to them, for they are the deer they hunt for. How many parishes in England (almost the number of half) have they empaled to themselves, and chased the Lord's deer out? Yea, now, if God lay challenge to his own ground, against their sacrilegious impropriations, for his own titles, they are not ashamed to tell him they are none of his ; and what laws soever he hath made, they will hold them with a *non obstante*. They were taken into the church for patrons, defenders ; and they prove offenders, thieves : for most often *patrocinia, latrocinia*.

You have read how the badger entertained the

101

hedgehog into his cabin as his inward friend; but, being wounded with the prickles of his offensive guest, he mannerly desired him to depart in kindness, as he came. The hedgehog thus satisfies his just expostulation: That he for his part found himself very well at ease, and they that were not had reason to seek out another place that likes them better. So the poor horse, entreating help of the man against the stag, ever after, *Non equitem dorso, non frænum depulit ore*,—They have rid us, and bridled us, and backed us, and spurred us, and got a tyranny over us, whom we took in for our familiar friends and favourites.

If you be disposed to hunt, hunt these beasts that havoc the commonwealth: let the lambs alone, they do much good, no hurt. And to this chase use all your skill; in this work it shall be your commendation to be cunning hunters. The Lord shall empark you within the pale of his own merciful providence, and restrain the savage fury of your enemies. Let those whom God hath made masters of this serious game, and given commission to hunt vicious persons, look to it. Let every particular man hunt vice out of his own heart. If there be any violence to get the kingdom of heaven, use it; if any policy to overthrow Satan and his accomplices, against whom we wrestle, exercise it. This war shall be your peace. You shall help to purge the land of noxious beasts, and cleanse your own hearts from those lusts, which if you hunt not to death shall hunt you to death ; as was the moral of Actæon. And God, that gives you this command and courage, shall add for it a merciful recompense ; taking you at last from this militant chase to the park of his triumphant rest. Amen.

HEAVEN MADE SURE

Say unto my soul, I am thy salvation.—
Psalm xxxv. 3.

THE words contain a petition for a benediction.
The supplicant is a king, and his humble suit is
to the King of kings : the king of Israel prays to
the King of heaven and earth.   He doth beg two
things :—1. That God would save him ; 2. That
God would certify him of it.   So that the text may
be distributed accordingly, into *salvation*, and the
assurance of it.

The *assurance* lies first in the words, and shall
have the first place in my discourse ; wherein I
conceive two things—the matter, and the manner.
The matter is *assurance;* the manner, *how*
assured : 'Say unto my soul.'

I.   From the matter, or *assurance*, observe—

1.   That salvation may be made sure to a man.
David would never pray for that which could not
be.   Nor would St Peter charge us with a duty
which stood not in possibility to be performed :
2 Pet. i. 10, ' Make your election sure.'   And to

stop the bawling throats of all cavilling adversaries,
Paul directly proves it : 2 Cor. xiii. 5, 'Know ye
not your own selves, how that Jesus Christ is in
you, except ye be reprobates?' We may then
know that Christ is in us : if Christ be in us, we
are in Christ ; if we be in Christ, we cannot be
condemned ; for, Rom. viii. 1, 'There is no damnation to them which are in Christ Jesus.'

2. That the best saints have desired to make
their salvation sure. David that knew it, yet
entreats to know it more. Ps. xli. 11, 'I know
thou favourest me'; yet here still, 'Say unto my
soul, I am thy salvation.' A man can never be
too sure of his going to heaven. If we purchase
an inheritance on earth, we make it as sure, and
our tenure as strong, as the brawn of the law, or
the brains of the lawyers, can devise. We have
conveyance, and bonds, and fines, no strength too
much. And shall we not be more curious in the
settling our eternal inheritance in heaven ? Even
the best certainty hath often, in this, thought itself
weak. Here we find matter of *consolation*, of
reprehension, of *admonition :* comfort to some,
reproof to others, warning to all.

Of *consolation*. Even David desires better
assurance : to keep us from dejection, behold,
they often think themselves weakest that are the

strongest. He calls himself the 'chiefest of sinners,' 1 Tim. i. 15, that was not the least of saints. Indeed sometimes a dear saint may want feeling of the spirit of comfort. Grace comes into the soul as the morning sun into the world: there is first a dawning, then a mean light, and at last the sun in his excellent brightness. In a Christian life there is *professio, profectio, perfectio.* A profession of the name of Christ wrought in our conversion; not the husk of religion, but the sap: 'A pure heart, a good conscience, and faith unfeigned.' Next, there is a profection, or going forward in grace, 'working up our salvation in fear and trembling.' Last, a perfection or full assurance, that we are 'sealed up to the day of redemption.'

And yet after this full assurance there may be some fear: it is not the commendation of this certainty to be void of doubting. The wealthiest saints have suspected their poverty; and the richest in grace are yet 'poorest in spirit.' As it is seen in rich misers: they possess much, yet esteem it little in respect of what they desire; for the fulness of riches cannot answer the insatiable affection. Whence it comes to pass that they have restless thoughts, and vexing cares for that they have not, not caring for that they have. So many good men, rich in the graces of God's

Spirit, are so desirous of more, that they regard
not what they enjoy, but what they desire:
complaining often that they have no grace, no
love, no life.

This is the sweetest comfort that can come to
a man in this life, even a heaven upon earth, to be
ascertained of his salvation.   There are many
mysteries in the world, which curious wits with
perplexful studies strive to apprehend.   But
without this, 'he that increaseth knowledge
increaseth sorrow,' Eccles. i. 18.   This one thing
is only necessary ; whatsoever I leave unknown,
let me know this, that I am the Lord's.   He may
without danger be ignorant of other things that
truly knows Jesus Christ.

There is no potion of misery so embittered
with gall but this can sweeten it with a comfortable
relish.   When enemies assault us, get us under,
triumph over us, imagining that salvation itself
cannot save us, what is our comfort?   'I know
whom I have believed' ; I am sure the Lord will not
forsake me.   Thou wantest bread ; God is thy
bread of life.   We want a pillow ; God is our
'resting-place,' Ps. xxxii. 7.   We may be without
apparel, not without faith; without meat, not without Christ; without a house, never without the Lord.
What state can there be wherein the stay of this
heavenly assurance gives us not peace and joy ?

107

Are we clapped up in a dark and desolate dungeon? there the light of the sun cannot enter, the light of mercy not be kept out. What restrained body, that hath the assurance of this eternal peace, will not pity the darkness of the profane man's liberty, or rather the liberty of his darkness? No walls can keep out an infinite spirit; no darkness can be uncomfortable where 'the Father of lights,' James i. 17, and the 'Sun of righteousness,' Mal. iv. 2, shineth. The presence of glorious angels is much, but of the most glorious God is enough.

Are we cast out in exile, our backs to our native home?—all the world is our way. Whither can we go from God? Ps. cxxxix. 7, 'Whither shall I go from thy face? or whither shall I flee from thy presence? If I ascend,' &c. That exile would be strange that could separate us from God. I speak not of those poor and common comforts, that in all lands and coasts it is his sun that shines, his elements of earth or water that bear us, his air we breathe; but of that special privilege, that his gracious presence is ever with us; that no sea is so broad as to divide us from his favour; that wheresoever we feed, he is our host; wheresoever we rest, the wings of his blessed providence are stretched over us. Let my soul be sure of this, though the whole world be traitors to me.

Doth the world despise us? We have sufficient recompense that God esteems us. How unworthy is that man of God's favour that cannot go away contented with it without the world's! Doth it hate us much? God hates it more. That is not ever worthy which man honours; but that is ever base which God despises. Without question, the world would be our friend if God were our enemy. The sweetness of both cannot be enjoyed; let it content us we have the best.

II. Thus much for the matter of the assurance, let us now come to the manner: 'Say unto my soul.'

SAY.—But is God a man? Hath he a tongue? How doth David desire him to speak? That God who made the ear, shall not he hear? He that made the eye, shall not he see? He that made the tongue, shall not he speak? He that sees without eyes, and hears without ears, and walks without feet, and works without hands, can speak without a tongue. Now God may be said to speak divers ways.

God speaks by *his Scriptures*: Rom. xv. 4, 'Whatsoever things were written aforetime were written for our learning, that we, through patience and comfort of the scriptures, might have hope.' *Scripta sunt,*—they are written. Things that go only by tale or tradition meet with such variations, augmentations, abbreviations, corruptions, false glosses, that, as in a lawyer's pleading, truth is lost in the *quære* for her. Related things we are long in getting, quick in forgetting ; therefore God commanded his law should be written. *Litera scripta manet.*

Thus God doth effectually speak to us. Many good wholesome instructions have dropped from human pens, to lesson and direct man in goodness ; but there is no promise given to any word to convert the soul but to God's word.

Oh that we had hearts to bless God for his mercy, that the Scriptures are among us, and that not sealed up under an unknown tongue ! The time was when a devout father was glad of a piece of the New Testament in English ; when he took his little son into a corner, and with joy of soul heard him read a chapter, so that even children became fathers to their fathers, and begat them to Christ. Now, as if the commonness had abated the worth, our Bibles lie dusty in the windows ; it is all if a Sunday-handling quit them from perpetual oblivion. Few can read, fewer do read, fewest of all read as they should. God of his infinite mercy lay not to our charge this neglect !

God speaks by *his ministers*, expounding and opening to us those Scriptures. These are *legati*

à latere,—dispensers of the mysteries of heaven ;
'ambassadors for Christ, as if God did beseech
you through us : so we pray you in Christ's stead,
that you would be reconciled to God,' 2 Cor. v. 20.
This voice is continually sounding in our churches,
beating upon our ears ; I would it could pierce
our consciences, and that our lives would echo to
it in an answerable obedience. How great should
be our thankfulness !

God hath dealt with us as he did with Elijah :
1 Kings xix. 11, 'The Lord passed by, and a
great and strong wind rent the mountains, and
brake in pieces the rocks before the Lord ; but
the Lord was not in the wind : after the wind
came an earthquake ; but the Lord was not in
the earthquake : after the earthquake a fire ; but
the Lord was not in the fire : and after the fire a
still voice' ; and the Lord came with that voice.
After the same manner hath God done to this
land. In the time of King Henry the Eighth,
there came a great and mighty wind, that rent
down churches, overthrew altarages, impropriated
from ministers their livings, that made laymen
substantial parsons, and clergymen their vicar-
shadows. It blew away the rights of Levi into
the lap of Issachar. A violent wind ; but God
was not in that wind. In the days of King Edward
the Sixth, there came a terrible earthquake,

hideous vapours of treasons and conspiracies, rumbling from Rome, to shake the foundations of that church, which had now left off loving the whore, and turned Antichrist quite out of his saddle. Excommunications of prince and people; execrations and curses in their tetrical forms with bell, book, and candle; indulgences, bulls, pardons, promises of heaven to all traitors that would extirpate such a king and kingdom. A monstrous earthquake; but God was not in the earthquake. In the days of Queen Mary came the fire, an unmerciful fire, such a one as was never before kindled in England, and, we trust in Jesus Christ, never shall be again. It raged against all that professed the gospel of Christ; made bonfires of silly women for not understanding that their ineffable mystery of transubstantiation; burnt the mother with the child. Bonner and Gardiner were those hellish bellows that set it on flaming. A raging and insatiable fire; but God was not in that fire. In the days of Queen Elizabeth, of blessed memory, came the still voice, saluting us with the songs of Sion, and speaking the comfortable things of Jesus Christ. And God came with this voice. This sweet and blessed voice is still continued by our gracious sovereign. God long preserve him with it, and it with him, and us all with them both!

To MY SOUL.—*Mine.* I might here examine
whose this *meæ* is. Who is the owner of this
my ? A prophet, a king, a man after God's own
heart ; that confessed himself the beloved of God ;
that knew the Lord would never forsake him ;
holy, happy David owns this *meæ :* he knows the
Lord loves him, yet desires to know it more ; Say
to *my* soul.

But let this teach us to make much of this *my*.
Luther says there is great divinity in pronouns.
The assurance that God will save some is a faith
incident to devils. The very reprobates may
believe that there is a book of election ; but God
never told them that their names were written
there. The hungry beggar at the feast-house gate
smells good cheer, but the master doth not say,
This is provided for thee. It is small comfort to
the harbourless wretch to pass through a goodly
city, and see many glorious buildings, when he
cannot say, I have a place here. The beauty of
that excellent city Jerusalem, built with sapphires,
emeralds, chrysolites, and such precious stones,
the foundation and walls whereof are perfect gold,
Rev. xxi., affords a soul no comfort, unless he can
say, I have a mansion in it. The all-sufficient
merits of Christ do thee no good, unless *tua pars
et portio*, he be thy Saviour. Happy soul that can
say with the Psalmist, 'O Lord, thou art my

portion!' Let us all have oil in our lamps, lest if
we be then to buy, beg, or borrow, we be shut out
of doors, like the fools, not worthy of entrance.

To conclude : it is salvation our prophet desires ;
that God would seal him up for his child, then
certify him of it. He requests not riches ; he knew
that man may be better fed than taught, that
wealth doth but frank men up to death. He that
prefers riches before his soul, doth but sell the
horse to buy the saddle, or kill a good horse to
catch a hare. He begs not honour : many have
leapt from the high throne to the low pit. The
greatest commander on earth hath not a foot of
ground in heaven, except he can get it by entitling
himself to Christ. He desires not pleasures ; he
knows there are as great miseries beyond prosperity as on this side it. And that all vanity is
but the indulgence of the present time ; a minute
begins, continues, ends it : for it endures but the
acting, and leaves no solace in the memory. In
the fairest garden of delights there is somewhat
that stings in the midst of all vain contents.

In a word, it is not momentary, variable, apt
to either change or chance, that he desires ; but
eternal salvation. He seeks, like Mary, 'that
better part which shall never be taken from him.'
The wise man's mind is ever above the moon,
saith Seneca : let the world make never so great

a noise, as if it all ran upon coaches, and all those full of roarers, yet all peace is there. It is not sublunary, under the wheel of changeable mortality, that he wishes, but salvation. To be saved is simply the best plot: beat your brains, and break your sleeps, and waste your marrows, to be wealthy, to be worthy—for riches, for honours; plot, study, contrive, be as politic as you can; and then kiss the child of your own brains, hug your inventions, applaud your wits, doat upon your advancements or advantagements; yet all these are but dreams. When you awake, you shall confess that to make sure your salvation was the best plot; and no study shall yield you comfort but what hath been spent about it. What should we then do but work and pray? 'Work,' saith Paul, Phil. ii. 12,—'Work up your salvation with fear and trembling'; and then pray with our prophet, 'Lord, say to our souls, thou art our salvation,' with comfort and rejoicing.

THE SINNER'S PASSING-BELL;

OR,

A COMPLAINT FROM HEAVEN FOR MAN'S SINS

Is there no balm in Gilead; is there no physician
there? why then is not the health of the
daughter of my people recovered?—

Jer. viii. 22.

THIS is a world to make physicians rich, if
men loved not their purse better than their health.
How few shalt thou meet, if their tongues would
be true to their griefs, without some disturbance
or affliction!   There lies one groaning of a sick
heart; another shakes his aching head; a third
roars for the torments of his reins; a fourth for
the racking of his gouty joints; a fifth grovels
with the falling sickness; a last lies half-dead of
a palsy.   Here is work for the physicians.   They
ruffle in the robes of preferment, and ride in the
foot-cloths of reverence.   Early and devout sup-
pliants stand at their study-doors, quaking, with
ready money in their hands, and glad it will be
accepted.   The body, if it be sick, is content

116

sometimes to buy leaden trash, with golden cash. But it is sick, and needs physic ; let it have it.

There is another physician, that thrives well too, if not best; and that is the lawyer. For men go not to the physician till their bodies be sick ; but to the lawyer when they be well, to make them sick. Thus, whiles they fear an ague, they fall into a consumption. He that scapes his disease and falls into the hands of his physicians, or from his trouble of suits lights into the fingers of his lawyer, fulfils the old verse—

'Incidit in Scyllam, dum vult vitare Charybdim';

physic gives wealth, and law honour. I speak not against due reward for just deserts in both these professions.

These physicians are both in request ; but the third, the physician of the soul, (of whom, I am now occasioned to shew, there is most need,) may stand at the door with Homer, and, did he speak with the voice of angels, not to be admitted. The sick rich man lies patiently under his physician's hands ; he gives him golden words, real thanks, nay, and often flattering observance.

But for the minister of his parish, if he may not have his head under his girdle, and his attendance as servile as his livery-groom's, he thinks himself indignified, and rages, like the Pope, that any priest durst eat of his peacock. How short doth this physician's respect fall of both the others! Let him 'feed his sheep,' John xxi. 16, if he will, with 'the milk of the word,' 1 Pet. ii. 2; his sheep will not feed him with the milk of reward. He shall hardly get from his patron the milk of the vicarage; but if he looks for the fleeces of the parsonage, he shall have, after the proverb, *lanam caprinam*, contempt and scorn.

Haman was not more mad for Mordecai's cap, Esther iii. 5, than the great one is, that as much observance ariseth not to him from the black coat as from his own blue coat. The church is beholden to him, that he will turn one of his cast servitors out of his own into her service; out of his chamber into the chancel; from the buttery-hatch to the pulpit. He that was not worthy enough to wait on his worship is good enough for God. Yield this sore almost healed, yet the honour of the ministry thrives like trees in autumn. Even their best estimate is but a shadow, and that a preposterous one; for it goes back faster than the shadow in the dial of Ahaz, Isa. xxxviii. 8. If a rich man have four sons, the youngest or contemnedst must be the priest. Perhaps the eldest shall be committed to his lands; for if his lands should be committed to him, his father fears he would carry them all up

to London: he dares not venture it without
binding it sure. For which purpose he makes
his second son a lawyer: a good rising profession,
for a man may by that (which I neither envy nor
tax) run up, like Jonah's gourd, to preferment;
and for wealth, a cluster of law is worth a whole
vintage of gospel. If he study means for his
third, lo, physic smells well; that, as the other
may keep the estate from running, so this the
body from ruining. For his youngest son he
cares not, if he puts him into God's service, and
makes him capable of the church-goods, though
not pliable to the church's good. Thus having
provided for the estate of his inheritance, of his
advancement, of his carcase, he comes last to
think of his conscience.

There is no herb to heal the wounds of the
soul, though you take the whole world for the
garden. All these professions are necessary, that
men's ignorance might not prejudice them, either
in wealth, health, or grace: God hath made men
fit with qualities, and famous in their faculties, to
preserve all these sound in us. The lawyer for
thy wealth, the physician for thy health, the
divine for thy soul. Physicians cure the body;
ministers the conscience.

The church of Israel is now exceeding sick;
and therefore the more dangerously, because she

knows it not. No physic is desired; therefore no health follows. She lies in a lethargy, and therefore speechless. She is so past sense of her weakness, that God himself is fain to ring her passing-bell. Aaron's bells cannot sound loud enough to waken her; God tolls from heaven a sad knell of complaint for her.

The words are divided to our hands by a rule of three. A tripartite metaphor, that willingly spreads itself into an allegory :—1. God's word is the balm; 2. The prophets are the physicians; 3. The people are the patients, who are very sick. Balm without a physician, a physician without balm, a patient without both, is an unhappy disjunction. If a man be ill, there is need of physic; when he hath physic, he needs a physician to apply it. So that, here is misery in being sick, mercy in the physic.

God leads us by sensible, to the sight of insensible wants; by calamities that vex our living bodies, to perils that endanger our dying consciences; that we might infer upon his premises what would be an eternal loss, by the sight of a temporal cross that is so hardly brooked. If a 'famine of bread' be so heavy, how unsupportable is the dearth of the word! saith the prophet, Amos viii. 11. Man may live without bread, not without the word, Matt. iv. 4. If a weary traveller

be so unable to bear a burden on his shoulders,
how ponderous is sin in the conscience! Matt.
xi. 28 : which Zechariah calls 'a talent of lead,'
chap. v. 7. If blindness be such a misery, what
is ignorance! If the night be so uncomfortable,
what doth the darkness of superstition afford! If
bodily disease so afflict our sense, how intolerable
will a spiritual sickness prove! Thus all earthly
and inferior objects to a Christian soul are like
marginal hands, directing his reading to a better
and heavenly reference. I intend to urge this
point the more, as it is more necessary, both for
the profit of it being well observed, and for the
general neglect of it ; because they are few in
these days that reduce Christianity to meditation,
but fewer that produce meditation to practice and
obedience.

It was God's usual dealing with Israel, by the
afflictions wherewith he grieved them, to put into
their minds how they had grieved him by their
sins. So Paul, as our prophet here, 'For this
cause ye are weak, sickly, and many die,' 1 Cor.
xi. 30 ; drawing them by these sensible cords of
their plagues to the feeling of their sins, which
made their souls faint in grace, sick in sin, dead
in apostasy. 'For this cause,' &c. This doctrine
affords a double use—particular and general ;
particular to ministers, general to all Christians.

To the dispensers of God's secrets. It allows them in borrowed forms to express the meditations of their hearts. God hath given us this liberty in the performance of our callings, not only nakedly to lay down the truth, but with the helps of invention, wit, art, to prevent the loathing of his manna. If we had none to hear us but Cornelius or Lydia, or such sanctified ears, a mere affirmation were a sufficient confirmation. But our auditors are like the Belgic armies, that consist of French, English, Scotch, German, Spanish, Italian, &c.; so many hearers, so many humours, the same diversity of men and minds : that as guests at a strange dish, every man hath a relish by himself; that all our helps can scarce help one soul to heaven. But of all kinds, there is none that creeps with better insinuation, or leaves behind it a deeper impression in the conscience, than a fit comparison. This extorted from David what would hardly have been granted : that as David slew Goliath with his own sword, so Nathan slew David's sin with his own word. Jotham convinced the Shechemites' folly in their approved reign of Abimelech over them, by the tale of the bramble, Judges ix. 8. Even temporal occasions open the mines to dig out spiritual instructions. The people flock to Christ for his bread; Christ preacheth to them another bread, whereof 'he that eats, shall never die,' John vi. 47. The Samaritan woman speaks to him of Jacob's well; he tells her of Jesus's well, John iv., whose bottom or foundation was in heaven, whose mouth and spring downwards to the earth, cross to all earthly fountains, containing 'water of life,' to be drawn and carried away in the buckets of faith. She thought it a new well, she found it a true well; whereof drinking, her soul's thirst was for ever satisfied. The cripple begs for an alms; the Apostle hath no money, but answers his small request with a great bequest—health 'in the name of the Lord Jesus,' Acts iii. 6. His purse is nothing the fuller, his body is much the happier. This course, you see, both Christ and his apostles gave us in practice and precept.

Physic and divinity are professions of a near affinity, both intending the cure and recovery, one of our bodies, the other and better, of our souls. Not that I would have them conjoined in one person; as one spake merrily of him that was both a physician and a minister, that whom he took money to kill by his physic, he had also money again to bury by his priesthood. Neither, if God hath poured both these gifts into one man, do I censure their union, or persuade their separation. Only, let the hound that runs after two hares at once take heed lest he catch neither.

And let him that is called into God's vineyard, *hoc agere*, 'attend on his office,' Rom. xii. 6—8. And beware, lest to keep his parish on sound legs, he let them walk with sickly consciences : whiles Galen and Avicen take the wall of Paul and Peter. I do not here tax, but rather praise, the works of mercy in those ministers that give all possible comforts to the distressed bodies of their brethren.

You see the willing similitude of these professions. Indeed, the physician cannot so aptly and ably challenge or make bold with the minister's office, as the minister may with his. The clergyman may minister medicines ; the physician may not administer the sacraments. It is true thus far. Every Christian is a priest to offer up prayers for himself and the whole church, although not publicly and ministerially. And if we 'serve one another in love,' we must carry, every one, a converting ministry, though God alone have the converting power : 'Turn one another, and live,' Ezek. xviii. 32. Now as this converting work is a convertible work,—I mean, reciprocal and mutual from one to another,—the physician may apportion to himself a great share in it. Who may better speak to the soul than he that is trusted with the body ? Or when can the stamp of grace take so easy impression in man's heart, as when the heat of God's affliction hath melted it? What breast is unvulnerable to the strokes of death? The miserable carcase hath, then or never, a penetrable conscience.

This conscience is so deafed in the days of our jollity, with the loud noise of music, oaths, carousings, clamours, quarrels, sports, that it cannot hear the prophet's cry, 'All flesh is grass.' When sickness hath thrown him on the bed of anguish, and made his stomach too queasy for quaffs, too fine and dainty for even junkets; naked him of his silks, paled his cheeks, sunk his eyes, chilled his blood, and stunted all his vigorous spirits; the physician is sent for, and must scarce be let out, when the minister may not be let in. His presence is too dull, and full of melancholy; no messenger shall come for him, till his coming be too late. How justly, then, should the physician be a divine, when the divine may not be a physician! How well may he mingle *recipe* and *resipisce*, penitential exhortations with his medicinal applications and prescripts!

If we take the words spoken in the person of the prophet, let us observe, that he is no good preacher that complains not in these sinful days. Isaiah had not more cause for Israel than we for England, to cry, 'We have laboured in vain, and spent our strength for nought,' chap. xlix. 4. For if we equal Israel in our blessings, we transcend them in our sins. The blood-red sea of war and slaughter, wherein other nations are drowned, as were the Egyptians, is become dry to our feet of peace. The bread of heaven, that true manna, satisfies our hunger, and our thirst is quenched with the waters of life. The better law of the gospel is given us ; and our saving health is not like a curious piece of arras folded up, but spread before our believing eyes, without any shadow cast over the beauty of it. We have a better High Priest, to make intercession for us in heaven, for whom he hath once sacrificed and satisfied on earth : with one act, with everlasting virtue. We want nothing that heaven can help us to, but that which we voluntarily will want, and without which we had better have wanted all the rest—thankfulness and obedience. We return God not one for a thousand, not a dram of service for so many talents of goodness. We give God the worst of all things, that hath given us the best of all things. We cull out the least sheaf for his tithe, the sleepiest hours for his prayers, the chippings of our wealth for his poor, a corner of the heart for his ark, when Dagon sits uppermost in our temple. He hath bowels of brass and a heart of iron, that cannot mourn at this our requital. We give God measure for measure, but after an ill manner. For his blessings, 'heapen, and shaken, and thrust together,' iniquities 'pressed down and yet running over.' Like hogs, we slaver his pearls, 'turn his graces into wantonness,' and turn again to rend in pieces the bringers.

If God complains against sin, let us not make ourselves merry with it. The mad humours, idle speeches, outrageous oaths of drunken atheists, are but ill mirth for a Christian spirit. Wickedness in others abroad should not be our tabret to play upon at home. It is a wretched thing to laugh at that which feasts Satan with mirth, laughing both at our sins, and at us for our sins.

Where are you, ye 'sons of the highest,' ye magistrates, put in power not only to lament our sins, but to take away the cause of our lamenting? Cease to beek yourselves, like Jehoiachim, before the fire of ease and rest; rend your clothes with Josiah, and wrap yourselves in sackcloth, like Nineveh's king, as a corpse laid out for burial. Do not, Felix-like, grope for a bribe in criminal offences; sell not your connivance, and withal your conscience, where you should give your punishment. Let not gold weigh heavier than Naboth's wrongs in the scales of justice. 'Weep, ye ministers, between the porch and the altar.'

Lament your own sins, ye inhabitants of the world. England, be not behind other nations in mourning, that art not short of them in offending. Religion is made but policy's stirrup, to get up and ride on the back of pleasure.

How should this make us mourn like doves, and groan like turtles! The wild swallows, our unbridled youngsters, sing in the warm chimneys; the lustful sparrows, noctivagant adulterers, sit chirping about our houses; the filching jays, secret thieves, rob our orchards; the kite and the cormorant devour and hoard our fruits; and shall not, among all these, 'the voice of the turtle be heard in our land,' Cant. ii. 12, mourning for these sinful rapines? Have whoredom and wine so taken away our hearts, and hidden them in a maze of vanities, that repentance cannot find them out? Can these enormities pass without our tears? Good men have not spent all their time at home in mourning for their own sins; sometimes they have judged it their work to lament what was others' work to do.

If I should set the mercies of our land to run along with Israel's, we should gain cope of them, and outrun them. And though in God's actual and outward mercies they might outstrip us, yet in his spiritual and saving health they come short of us. They had the shadow, we the substance:

they candle-light, we noon-day : they the breakfast of the law, fit for the morning of the world ;
we the dinner of the gospel, fit for the high noon
thereof.

Look round about you, and whiles you quake
at the plagues so natural to our neighbours, bless
your own safety and our God for it.   Behold the
confines of Christendom, Hungary and Bohemia,
infested and wasted with the Turks ; Italy groaning
under the slavery of Antichrist, which infects the
soul worse than the Turk infests the body.   Behold
the pride of Spain, curbed with a bloody Inquisi-
tion ; France, a fair and flourishing kingdom,
made wretched by her civil uncivil wars. Germany
knew not of long time what peace meant ; neither
is their war ended, but suspended.   Ireland hath
felt the perpetual plague of her rebellions ; and
Scotland hath not wanted her fatal disasters.
Only England hath lain, like Gideon's fleece, dry
and secure, when the rain of judgments hath
wetted the whole earth.   When God hath tossed
the nations, and made them 'like a wheel,' and
'as the stubble before the wind,' Ps. lxxxiii. 13,
only England that hath stood like Mount Zion,
with unmoved firmness.   Time was she petitioned
to Rome ; now she neither fears her bulls nor
desires her bulwarks. The barbarous are now
unfeared enemies, and the sea is rather our fort

than our sepulchre. A peaceful prince leads us, and the 'Prince of peace' leads him. And besides our peace, we are so happy for balm and physicians, that if I should sing of the blessings of God to us, this should still be the burden of my song, 'What could the Lord do more for us?'

'There is balm in Gilead, there are physicians there.' Will there be ever so? Is there not a time to lose as well as to get? If whiles the sanctuary is full of this holy balm, God's word; if whiles there is plenty of physicians, and in them plenty of skill, 'the health of Israel is not restored,' how dangerous will her sickness be in the privation of both these restoratives? They that grow not rich in peace, what will they do in war? He that cannot live well in summer, will hardly scape starving in winter. Israel, that once had her cities sown with prophets, could after say, 'We see not our signs, there is not one prophet among us.' They that whilom loathed manna, would have been glad if, after many a weary mile, they could have tasted the crumbs of it. He whose prodigality scorned the 'bread in his father's house,' would afterwards have thought himself refreshed with 'the husks for the swine.'

The sun doth not ever shine; there is a time of setting. No day of jollity is without his evening of conclusion, if no cloud of disturbance prevent it with an overcasting. First God complains, men sing, dance, are jovial and neglectful; at last man shall complain, and 'God shall laugh at their destructions.' Why should God be conjured to receive that spirit dying that would not receive God's Spirit living? All things are whirled about in their circular courses, and who knows whether the next spoke of their wheel will not be a blank?

Lastly, observe, there is balm and physicians. What is the reason, saith God, that 'my people's health is not recovered'? Would you know why Israel is not recovered by these helps? Let your meditations go along with me, and I will shew you the reasons why God's physic works not on her:—

She knew not her own sickness. We say, the first step to health is to know that we are sick. The disease being known, it is half cured. This is the difference betwixt a fever and a lethargy: the one angers the sense, but doth keep it quick, tender, and sensible; the other obstupefies it. The lethargised is not less sick because he complains not so loud as the aguish. He is so much the nearer his own end, as he knows not that his disease is begun. Israel was sick, and knew it not; or, as Christ said of the Pharisees, would not know it. There is no surer course for the devil to work his pleasure on men than to keep them in ignorance. How easily doth that thief rob and spoil the house of our souls, when he hath first put out the candle of knowledge! Who wonders if the blind man cannot see the shining sun? When Antiochus entered to the spoil of the sanctuary, the first things he took away were the golden altar and the candlestick of light, 1 Macc. i. 21. When the devil comes to rifle God's spiritual temple, man's soul, the first booty that he lays his sacrilegious hands on are sacrifice and knowledge, the altar and the lamp. That subtle falconer knows that he could not so quietly carry us on his fist, without baiting and striving against him, if we were not hooded.

Thus wretched is it for a man not to see his wretchedness. Such a one spends his days in a dream; and goes from earth to hell, as Jonah from Israel toward Tarshish, fast asleep. This Paul calls the 'cauterised conscience'; which when the devil, an ill surgeon, would sear up, he first casts his patient into a mortiferous sleep. And, that all the noise which God makes by his ministers, by his menaces, by his judgments, might not waken him, Satan gives him some opium, an ounce of security, able to cast Samson himself into a slumber, especially when he may lay his voluptuous head on the lap of Delilah.

Israel is then sick in sin, and yet thinks herself righteous.

The last defect of Israel's cure is the want of application. What should a sick man do with physic, when he lets it fust in a vessel, or spills it on the ground? It is ill for a man to mispose that to loss which God hath disposed to his good. Beloved, application is the sweet use to be made of all sermons. In vain to you are our ministries of God's mysteries, when you open not the doors of your hearts to let them in. In vain we smite your rocky hearts, when you pour out no floods of tears. In vain we thunder against your sins, covetous oppressions of men, treacherous rebellions against God, when no man says, 'Master, is it I?' Is that spoken to no man which is spoken to all men? Whiles covetousness is taxed, not one of twenty churls lays his finger on his own sore. Whiles lust is condemned, what adulterer feels the pulse of his own conscience? Whiles malice is inquired of in the pulpit, there is not a Nabalish neighbour in the church will own it. It is our common armour against the sword of the Spirit: It is not to me he speaks. For which God at last gives them an answerable plague: they shall as desperately put from them all the comforts of the gospel, as they have presumptuously rejected all the precepts of the law. They that would apply no admonition to themselves, nor take one grain out of the whole heap of doctrines for their own use, shall at last, with an invincible forwardness, bespeak themselves every curse in the sacred volume.

Thus easy and ordinary is it for men to be others' physicians, rather than their own ; statesmen in foreign commonwealths, not looking into their own doors ; sometimes putting on Aaron's robes, and teaching him to teach ; and often scalding their lips in their neighbours' pottage. They can weed others' gardens, whiles their own is overrun with nettles ; like that soldier that digged a fountain for Cæsar, and perished himself in a voluntary thirst. But charity begins at home ; and he that loves not his own soul, I will hardly trust him with mine. The usurer blames his son's pride, sees not his own extortion ; and whiles the hypocrite is helping the dissolute out of the mire, he sticks in deeper himself. The Pharisees are on the disciples' jacket for eating with unwashen hands, whiles themselves are not blameworthy that eat with unwashen hearts. No marvel if, when we fix both our eyes on others' wants, we lack a third to see our own. If two blind men rush one upon another in the way, either complains of the other's blindness, neither of his own. Thus, like mannerly guests, when a good morsel is carved us, we lay it liberally on another's trencher, and fast ourselves. How much better were it for us to feed on our own portion!

Go back, go back, thou foolish sinner; turn in to thine own house, and stray not with Dinah till thou be ravished. 'Consider your ways in your hearts,' Hag. i. 5. If thou findest not work enough to do at home, in cleansing thy own heart, come forth then and help thy neighbours. Whosoever you are, sit not like lookers-on at God's mart; but having good wares proffered you, and that so cheap, —'grace, peace,' and remission of sins for nothing, —take it, and bless his name that gives it. Receive with no less thankfulness the physic of admonition he sends you; apply it carefully: if it do not work on your souls effectually, there is nothing left that may do you good. The word of God is powerful as his own majesty, and shall never return back to himself again without speeding the commission it went for. Apply it, then, to your souls in faith and repentance, lest God apply it in fear and vengeance. Lord, open our hearts with the key of grace, that thy holy word may enter in, to reign in us in this world, and to save us in the world to come! Amen.

GOD'S HOUSE;

OR,

THE PLACE OF PRAISES

I will go into thy house with burnt-offerings :
I will pay thee my vows.—Psalm lxvi. 13.

THE matter and substance of the verse is
thankfulness ; the manner and form, resolution.
The whole fabric declares the former ; the fashion
of the building, the latter.   The tenor of all is
praising God ; the key of tune it is set in,
purpose : ' I will go into thy house ; I will pay
thee my vows.'   So that first I must entreat you
to look upon a solution and a resolution ; a debt
to be paid, and a purpose of heart to pay it.

The DEBT is thankfulness.   This is the matter
and substance of the words.   God having first,
by affliction, taught us to know ourselves, doth
afterwards, by deliverance, teach us to know him.
And when his gracious hand hath helped us out
of the low pit, he looks that, like Israel, Exod. xv.,
we should stand upon the shore and bless his
name.   David, that prayed to God *de profundis*,
Ps. cxxx. 1, ' Out of the depths have I called

136

unto thee,' doth after praise him *in excelsis*, with
the highest organs and instruments of laud.

General mercies require our continual thanks,
but new favours new praises. Ps. xcviii. 1, 'O
sing unto the Lord a new song, for he hath done
marvellous things.' There is a fourfold life be-
longing to man, and God is the keeper of all: his
natural, civil, spiritual, and eternal life. Bloody
man would take away our natural life, (Ps. xxxvii.
32, 'The wicked watcheth the righteous, and
seeketh to slay him';) God keeps it. The slanderous world would blast our civil life; God
blesseth our memory. The corrupted flesh would
poison our spiritual life; God 'hides it in Christ,'
Col. iii. 3. The raging devil would kill our eternal
life; God preserves it in heaven. Unworthy are
we of rest that night wherein we sleep, or of the
light of the sun that day wherein we rise, without
praising God for these mercies. If we think not
on him that made us, we think not to what
purpose he made us.

I come from the debt to be paid, to his
resolution to pay it: 'I will go into thy house; I
will pay,' &c. Though he be not instantly
solvendo, he is *resolvendo*. He is not like those
debtors that have neither means nor meaning to
pay. But though he wants actual, he hath votal
retribution. Though he cannot so soon come to

137

the place where this payment is to be made, yet he hath already paid it in his heart : 'I will go ; I will pay.'   Here, then, is the debtor's

RESOLUTION.—There is in the godly a purpose of heart to serve the Lord.   This is the child of a sanctified spirit, born not without the throbs and throes of true penitence.   Not a transient and perishing flower, like Jonah's gourd,—*filius noctis; oriens, moriens,*—but the sound fruit, which the sap of grace in the heart sends forth.   Luke xv. 18, when the prodigal son 'came to himself,' saith the text,—as if he had been formerly out of his wits,—his first speech was, 'I will arise, and go to my father, and will say unto him, Father, I have sinned.'   And what he purposed, he performed : he rose and went.

I know there are many that intend much, but do nothing ; and that earth is full of good purposes, but heaven only full of good works ; and that the tree gloriously leaved with intentions, without fruit, was cursed ; and that a lewd heart may be so far smitten and convinced at a sermon, as to will a forsaking of some sin.   Which thoughts are but swimming notions, and vanishing motions ; embryons, or abortive births.

David's first care is to visit God's house.   It is very likely that this psalm was written by David either in exile under Saul, or in persecution

by Absalom, or in some grievous distress; where-
out being delivered, he first resolves to salute
God's house. Chrysostom *in Opere Imperfecto*,
or whosoever was the author of that book, notes
it the property of a good son, when he comes to
town, first to visit his father's house, and to
perform the honour that is due to him. We find
this in Christ. Matt. xxi. 10–12, so soon as ever
he came to Jerusalem, first he visits his Father's
house : 'He went into the temple.' What the
Son and Lord of David did there, the same
course doth the servant of his Son take here :
first, 'I will go into thy house.'

Oh for one dram of this respect of God's
house in these days! Shall that place have a
principal place in our affections? We would not
then think one hour tedious in it, when many
years delight us in the 'tents of Kedar.' This
was not David's opinion : Ps. lxxxiv. 10, 'One
day in thy courts is better than a thousand.' Nor
grudge at every penny that a levy taxeth to the
church, as if *tegumen parietibus impositum* was
enough,—bare walls, and a cover to keep us from
rain ; and *aliquid ornatus* was but superfluous,
except it be a cushion and a wainscot seat, for a
gentleman's better ease. The greatest preparation
usually against some solemn feast is but a little
fresh straw under the feet, the ordinary allowance

139

for hogs in the stye or horses in the stable. For other cost, let it be a cage of unclean birds ; and so it must be so long as some sacrilegious persons are in it. It was part of the epitaph of King Edgar—He gave temples to God, ministers to those temples, and maintenance to those ministers. But the epitaphs of too many in these days may well run in contrary terms. They take tenths from good ministers, good ministers from the churches, yea, and some of them also the churches from God.

I might here take just cause to tax an error of our times. Many come to these holy places, and are so transported with a desire of hearing, that they forget the fervency of praying and praising God. The end is ever held more noble than the means that conduce unto it. Sin brought in ignorance, and ignorance takes away devotion. The word preached brings in knowledge, and knowledge rectifies devotion. So that all our preaching is but to beget your praying ; to instruct you to praise and worship God. The most immediate and proper service and worship of God is the end, and hearing but the means to that end.

I complain not that our churches are auditories, but that they are not oratories ; not that you come to sermons, (for God's sake, come faster,) but that you neglect public prayer : as if it were only God's part to bless you, not yours to bless God. And hereof I complain with good company. Chrysostom saith, that such a multitude came to his sermons, that there was scarce room for a late comer ; and those would all patiently attend the end of the sermon : but when prayers were to be read, or sacraments to be administered, the company was thin, the seats empty.

Beloved, mistake not. It is not the only exercise of a Christian to hear a sermon ; nor is that Sabbath well spent that despatcheth no other business for heaven. I will be bold to tell you, that in heaven there shall be no sermons ; and yet in heaven there shall be hallelujahs. And this same end, for which David came to God's house, shall remain in glory—to praise the Lord. So that all God's service is not to be narrowed up in hearing, it hath greater latitude ; there must be prayer, praise, adoration, and worship of God. Neither is it the scope of Christianity to know, but the scope of knowledge is to be a good Christian.

We perceive now the motive-cause that brought David into God's house. I would take leave from hence in a word to instruct you with what mind you should come to this holy place. We are in substance inheritors of the same faith which the

Jews held ; and have—instead of their tabernacle,
sanctuary, temple—churches, places set apart for
the assembly of God's saints ; wherein we receive
divine mysteries, and celebrate divine ministries.
There is nothing lost by the gospel which the law
afforded ; but rather all bettered. It is observable
that the building of that glorious temple was the
maturity and consummation of God's mercy to the
Jews. Infinite were his favours betwixt their
slavery in Egypt and their peace in Israel. God
did, as it were, attend upon them to supply their
wants. They have no guide : why, God himself
is their guide, and goes before them in a pillar of
fire. They have no shelter : the Lord spreads a
cloud over them for a canopy. Are they at a
stand, and want way? The sea shall part and
give them passage, whilst the divided waters are
as walls unto them. For sustenance, they lack
bread : heaven itself shall pour down the food of
angels. Have they no meat to their bread? A
wind shall blow to them innumerable quails.
Bread and flesh is not enough without drink :
behold, a hard rock, smitten with a little wand,
shall pour out abundance of water. But what is
all this, if they yet in the wilderness shall want
apparel? Their garments shall not wax old on
their backs. Do they besiege? Jericho's walls
shall fall down before them ; for want of engines,

hailstones shall brain their enemies; lamps, and pitchers, and dreams shall get them victory. 'The sun shall stand still on Gibeon, and the moon in the valley of Ajalon,' Josh. x. 12, to behold their conquests. Lack they yet a land to inhabit? The Lord will make good his promise against all difficulties, and give them a land that 'flows with milk and honey.'

But is all this yet short of our purpose, and their chief blessedness? They want a house to celebrate his praise that hath done all this for them: behold, the Lord giveth them a goodly temple; neither doth he therein only accept their offerings, but he also gives them his oracles, even vocal oracles between the cherubims. I might easily parallel England to Israel in the circumference of all these blessings; but my centre is their last and best, and whereof they most boasted: Jer. vii. 4, 'The temple of the Lord,' and the law of their God. To answer these we have the houses of God, and the gospel of Jesus Christ. We have all, though all in a new manner: 2 Cor. v. 17, 'Old things are passed away; behold, all things are become new.' They had an 'Old Testament,' Heb. viii. 13; we have the 'New Testament.' They had the Spirit; we have a new Spirit. They had commandments; we have the 'new commandment,' John xiii. 34. They had an inheri-

tance, Canaan; we have a new inheritance
promised: Rev. xxi. 1, 'I saw a new heaven and
a new earth.' To conclude, they had their temple,
we have our churches; to which as they were
brought by their sabbath, so we by our Lord's
day; wherein as they had their sacraments, so we
have our sacraments. We must therefore bear
the like affection to ours as they did to that.
We have greater cause. There was the shadow,
here is the substance; there the figure, here the
truth; there the sacrifices of beasts, here of 'the
Lamb of God taking away the sin of the world.'

It is holy ground, not by any inherent holiness,
but in regard of the religious use. For that
place which was once *Bethel*, the house of God,
proved afterward *Bethaven*, the house of iniquity.
But it is thus God's sanctuary, the habitation of
his sanctity: 'Put off thy shoes,'—doff thy carnal
affections,—'the place where thou standest is holy
ground'; 'wash thy hands,' yea, thy heart, 'in
innocency,' before thou 'come near to God's altar.'
Be the minister never so simple, never so sinful,
the word is holy, the action holy, the time holy,
the place holy, ordained by the Most Holy to
make us holy. Saith a reverend divine, God's
house is for godly exercises; they wrong it, therefore, that turn *sanctuarium* into *promptuarium*,
the sanctuary into a buttery, and spiritual food,

into belly-cheer. And they much more, that pervert it to a place of pastime, making the house of praise a house of plays. And they most of all, that make it a house, not *laudis*, but *fraudis*,—Matt. xxi. 13, 'My house is the house of prayer but ye have made it a den of thieves,'—robbing, if not men of their goods, yet God of the better part, sincerity of conscience.

What a horrid thing would it be, beloved, if you should depart from this church, where you learn to keep a good conscience, but into the market, and there practise deceit, circumvention, oppression, swearing, drunkenness! Oh, do not derive the commencement of your sins from God's house! What a mockery is this, and how odious in the sight of heaven, if you should begin your wickedness with a sermon, as the Papists begin their treasons with a mass! I tax no known person; but for the facts and faults, I do not speak of things unknown. I would to God your amended lives might bring me with shame again hither to recant and unsay it.

But it often so falls out, that as those conspirators met at the Capitol, so the church is made the *communis terminus*, where many wickednesses have appointed to meet. 'What agreement hath the temple of God with idols?' 2 Cor. vi. 16. Begin not the day with God, to spend all the rest

with Satan. Your tongues have now blessed the
Lord; let not the evening find them red with
oaths, or black with curses. Let not that saying
of Luther be verified by you, that in the name
of God begins all mischief. Whatsoever your
morning sacrifice pretend, look to your afternoon.
You have done so much the worse, as you have
made a show of good; and it had been easier
for your unclean hearts to have missed this
admonition. This caveat, before I leave God's
house, I thought to commend to your practice,
when you leave it.

There are some so far from refusers, that they
are rather intruders. They will come into God's
house, but they will bring no burnt-offerings with
them; no preparation of heart to receive benefit
in the church. They come without their wedding-
garment, and shall one day hear that fearful and
unanswerable question, 'Friends, how came you
in hither?'

These are the utterly profane, that come rather
with a lame knowledge than a blind zeal. For
some of them, good clothes carry them to church;
and they had rather men should note the fashion
of their habits than God the habit of their hearts.
They can better brook ten disorders in their lives
than one in their locks. Others are the secure
semi-atheistical cosmopolites; and these come

too : and none take a truer measure of the sermon, for their sleep begins with the prayer before it, and wakens just at the psalm after it. These think that God may be served well enough with looking on ; and their utmost duty, but to bring their bodies a little further living than they shall be brought dead : for then perhaps they shall come to the churchyard, now they will bring them to the church. Devotion and they are almost strangers, and so much as they know of it, they dishonour by their acquaintance. Their burnt-offerings are nothing else but a number of eyes at utmost lift up to heaven ; their heart hath another centre. They bring as many sins with them every day to church as they have been all their lives in committing. Their hands are not washed from aspersions of lust and blood ; their eyes are full of whoredom; their lips of slander, their affections of covetousness, their wits of cheating, their souls of impiety. If there were no saints in the church, how could they hope the roof would not fall on their guilty heads? But I will leave them to the Lord's reproof : Jer. vii. 9–11, 'Will ye steal, murder, commit adultery, and swear falsely ; and come and stand before me in this house,' staring me in the face, as if you were innocent ? 'Behold, even I have seen it, saith the Lord.'

There is yet a last sort, that will come into God's house, and bring with them burnt-offerings, a show of external devotion ; but they will not pay their vows. Distress, war, captivity, calamity, famine, sickness, brings down the most elate and lofty spirits. It turns the proud gallant's feather into a kerchief; pulls the wine from the lips of the drunkard ; ties up the tongue of the swearer, whom thunder could not adjure to silence ; makes the adulterer loathe the place of his sin, the bed. And though the usurer stuff his pillow with nothing but his bonds and mortgages, softer and sweeter in his opinion than down or feathers, yet his head will not leave aching.

This misery doth so sting, terrify, and put sense into the dead flesh of the numbed conscience, that (all worldly delights being found like plummets of lead tied about a man while he is cast into this sea, so far from helping him to swim, that they sink him rather,) the eye looks about for another shore, and finds none but God. To this so long forgotten God, the heart begins to address a messenger, and that is prayer. God, the wicked see, must be called on, but they know not how. They have been so mere strangers to him, that they cannot tell how to salute him. Like beggars that are blind, they are forced to beg, but they see not of whom. The Lord no sooner takes off the

burden of misery, but we also shake off the burden
of piety ; we forget our vows. Oh the mercy of
God, that such forgetfulness should possess
Christian hearts ! This was unthankful Israel's
fault: Ps. cvi. 13, 'They soon forgat his works' ;
they forgat, yea, soon ; they made haste to forget,
so the original is : 'They made haste, they forgat.'
Like men that in sleep shake Death by the hand,
but when they are awake will not know him.

It is storied of a merchant, that in a great
storm at sea he vowed to Jupiter, if he would save
him and his vessel, to give him a hecatomb. The
storm ceaseth, and he bethinks that a hecatomb
was unreasonable ; he resolves on seven oxen.
Another tempest comes, and now he vows again
the seven at least. Delivered then also, he
thought that seven were too many, and one ox
would serve the turn. Yet another peril comes,
and now he vows solemnly to fall no lower ; if
he might be rescued, an ox Jupiter shall have.
Again freed, the ox sticks in his stomach, and
he would fain draw his devotion to a lower rate ;
a sheep was sufficient. But at last, being set
ashore, he thought a sheep too much, and purposeth to carry to the altar only a few dates. But
by the way he eats up the dates, and lays on the
altar only the shells. After this rate do many
perform their vows. They promise whole heca-

149

tombs in sickness, but they reduce them lower and lower still as they grow well. He that vowed to build an hospital, to restore an impropriation to the church, to lay open his enclosures, and to serve God with an honest heart, brings all at last to a poor reckoning, and thinks to please the Lord with his empty shells. There was some hope of this man's soul's health while his body was sick; but as his body riseth to strength, his soul falls to weakness.

You see all the parts of this song; the whole concert or harmony of all is praising God. I have shewed you *quo loco*, in his house; *quo modo*, with burnt-offerings; *quo animo*, paying our vows. Time hath abridged this discourse, contrary to my promise and purpose.

In a word, which of us is not infinitely beholden to the Lord our God, for sending to us many good things, and sending away from us many evil things? Oh, where is our praise, where is our thankfulness? 'What shall we do unto thee, O thou preserver of men?' What but 'take the cup of salvation, and bless the name of the Lord'? Ps. c. 4, 'Oh, let us enter into his gates with thanksgiving, and into his courts with praise: let us be thankful unto him, and bless his name.' And let us not bring our bodies only, but our hearts; let our souls be thankful.

GOD'S HOUSE

Man's body is closed up within the elements :
his blood within his body, his spirits in his blood,
his soul within his spirits, and the Lord resteth in
his soul. Let then the soul praise the Lord ; let
us not draw near with our lips, and leave our
hearts behind us ; but let us give the Searcher of
the hearts a hearty praise. Ingratitude is the
devil's text ; oaths, execrations, blasphemies, and
lewd speeches are commentaries upon it. But
thankfulness is the language of heaven ; for it
becometh saints to be thankful. As therefore we
would give testimony to the world, and argument
to our own conscience, that we serve the Lord, let
us promise and perform the words of my text,
'We will go into thy house with burnt-offerings :
we will pay thee our vows.' The Lord give
thankfulness to us, and accept it of us, for Jesus
Christ's sake ! Amen.

THE SINNER'S MOURNING-HABIT

Wherefore I abhor myself and repent in dust and ashes.—Job xlii. 6.

AFFLICTION is a winged chariot, that mounts up the soul toward heaven; nor do we ever so rightly understand God's majesty as when we are not able to stand under our own misery. It was Naaman's leprosy that brought him to the knowledge of the prophet, and the prophet brought him to the saving knowledge of the true God. Had he not been a leper, he had still been a sinner. *Schola crucis, schola lucis,*—there is no such school instructing as the cross afflicting. If Paul had not been buffeted by Satan, he might have gone nigh to buffet God, through danger of being puffed up with his revelations.

The Lord hath many messengers by whom he solicits man. He sends one health, to make him a strong man; another wealth, to make him a rich man; another sickness, to make him a weak man; another losses, to make him a poor man; another age, to make him an old man; another death, to make him no man. But among

them all, none despatcheth the business surer or
sooner than affliction ; if that fail of bringing a
man home, nothing can do it. He is still importunate for an answer ; yea, he speaks, and
strikes. Do we complain of his incessant blows ?
Alas ! he doth but his office, he waits for our
repentance ; let us give the messenger his errand,
and he will begone. Let him take the proud man
in hand, he will humble him : he can make the
drunkard sober, the lascivious chaste, the angry
patient, the covetous charitable ; fetch the unthrift
son back again to his father, whom a full purse
had put into an itch of travelling, Luke xv. 17.

Job was not ignorant of God before, while he
sat in the sunshine of peace ; but resting his head
on the bosom of plenty, he could lie at his ease
and contemplate the goodness of his Maker. But
as when the sun shines forth in his most glorious
brightness, we are then least able to look upon
him,—we may solace ourselves in his diffused rays
and comfortable light, but we cannot fix our eyes
upon that burning carbuncle,—these outward
things do so engross us, take up our consideration,
and drown our contemplative faculty in our sense,
that so long we only observe the effects of God's
goodness, rather than the goodness of God itself.
Necessity teacheth us the worth of a friend ; as
absynthium (wormwood) rubbed upon the eyes

153

makes them smart a little, but they see the clearer. Therefore Job confessed that in his prosperity he had only, as it were, heard of God ; but now in his trial he had seen him. Such a more full and perfect apprehension of God did calamity work in this holy man ; and from that speculation proceeds this humiliation, 'Wherefore I abhor myself, and repent in dust and ashes.'

In spiritual graces let us study to be great, and not to know it, as the fixed stars are every one bigger than the earth, yet appear to us less than torches. *In alto non altum sapere*, not to be high-minded in high deserts, is the way to blessed preferment. Humility is not only a virtue itself, but a vessel to contain other virtues : like embers, which keep the fire alive that is hidden under it. It emptieth itself by a modest estimation of its own worth, that Christ may fill it. It wrestleth with God, like Jacob, and wins by yielding ; and the lower it stoops to the ground, the more advantage it gets to obtain the blessing. All our pride, O Lord, is from the want of knowing thee. O thou infinite Maker, reveal thyself yet more unto us ; so shall we 'abhor ourselves, and repent in dust and ashes.'

The children of grace have learned to think well of other men and to abhor themselves. And indeed when we consider what master we have

served, and what wages deserved, we have just
cause to abhor ourselves. What part of us hath
not sinned, that it should not merit to be despised?
Run all over this little Isle of Man, and find me
one member of the body, or faculty of the soul,
that can say with Job's messenger—'I alone have
escaped.' Where is that innocency which desires
not to stand only in the sight of mercy? What
time, what place are not witnesses against us?
The very Sabbath, the day of rest, hath not rested
from our evils. The very temple, that holy place,
hath been defiled with our obliquities. Our
chambers, our beds, our boards, the ground we
tread, the air we breathe, can tell our follies.
There is no occasion which, if it do not testify
what evil we have done, yet can say what good
we should and have not done. How far soever
we have run out, we hope to make all reckonings
even when repentance comes; but what if repentance never comes?

It is not many years, more incitations, and
abundance of means, that can work it; but repentance is the fair gift of God. One would think
it a short lesson, yet Israel was forty years a-
learning it; and they no sooner got it but presently
forgot it. Rev. xvi. 11, we read of men plagued
with heat, and pains, and sores, yet they repented
not. Judas could have a broken neck, not a broken

heart. There is no such inducement to sin as the presumption of ready repentance, as if God had no special riches of his own, but every sinner might command them at his pleasure. The king hath earth of his own, he lets his subjects walk upon it ; he hath a sea, lets them sail on it ; his land yields fruit, lets them eat it ; his fountains water, lets them drink it. But the moneys in his exchequer, the garments in his wardrobe, the jewels in his jewel-house, none may meddle with but they to whom he disposeth them. God's common blessings are not denied ; his sun shines, his rain falls, Matt. v. 45, on the righteous and unrighteous. But the treasures of heaven, the robes of glory, the jewels of grace and repentance, these he keeps in his own hands, and gives not where he may, but where he will. Man's heart is like a door with a spring-lock ; pull the door after you, it locks of itself, but you cannot open it again without a key. Man's heart doth naturally lock out grace ; none but he that 'hath the key of the house of David,' Rev. iii. 7, can open the door and put it in. God hath made a promise to repentance, not of repentance ; we may trust to that promise, but there is no trusting to ourselves. Nature flatters itself with that singular instance of mercy, one malefactor on the cross repenting at his last hour. But such hath been Satan's policy, to draw evil out of good, that the calling and saving of that one soul hath been the occasion of the loss of many thousands.

Wheresoever repentance is, she doth not deliberate, tarries not to ask questions and examine circumstances, but bestirs her joints, calls her wits and senses together; summons her tongue to praying, her feet to walking, her hands to working, her eyes to weeping, her heart to groaning. There is no need to bid her go, for she runs; she runs to the word for direction, to her own heart for remorse and compunction, to God for grace and pardon; She resolves that her knees shall grow to the pavement, till mercy hath answered her from heaven. As if she had felt an earthquake in her soul, not unlike that jailor when he felt the foundations of his prison shaken, she 'calls for a light,' Acts xvi. 29, the gospel of truth, and springs in trembling; and the first voice of her lips is, ' O what shall I do to be saved?' She lows with mourning, like the kine that carried the ark, and never rests till she comes to Bethshemesh, the fields of mercy. The good star that guides her is the promise of God; this gives her light through all the dark clouds of her sorrow. Confidence is her life and soul; she draws no other breath than the persuasion of mercy, that the 'king of Israel is a merciful king,' 1 Kings xx. 31. Faith is the

heart-blood of repentance. The matter, composition, constitution, substance of it, is amend-
ment of life; there be many counterfeits that walk
in her habit, as King Ahab had his shadows, but
that is her substance. Her countenance is spare
and thin; she hath not eyes standing out with
fatness. Her diet is abstinence; her garment
and livery, sackcloth and ashes; the paper
in her hand is a petition; her dialect is *Miserere*;
and lest her own lusts should be bane within
her, she sweats them out with confession and
tears.

We know there is no other fortification against
the judgments of God but repentance. His forces
be invisible, invincible; not repelled with sword
and target; neither portcullis nor fortress can
keep them out; there is nothing in the world that
can encounter them but repentance. They had
long since laid our honour in the dust, rotted our
carcases in the pit, sunk our souls into hell, but
for repentance. Which of those saints, that are
now saved in heaven, have not sinned upon earth?
What could save them but repentance? If I
should give you the picture of repentance, I would
tell you that she is a virgin fair and lovely; and
those tears, which seem to do violence to her
beauty, rather indeed grace it. Her breast is sore
with the strokes of her own penitent hands, which

are always either in Moses's posture in the mount,
lift up towards heaven, or the publican's in the
temple, smiting her bosom. Her knees are
hardened with constant praying; her voice is
hoarse with calling to heaven; and when she
cannot speak, she delivers her mind in groans.
There is not a tear falls from her, but an angel
holds a bottle to catch it. She thinks every
man's sins less than her own, every man's good
deeds more. Her compunctions are unspeakable,
known only to God and herself. She could wish,
not only men, but even beasts, and trees, and
stones, to mourn with her. She thinks no sun
should shine, because she takes no pleasure in it;
that the lilies should be clothed in black, because
she is so apparelled. Mercy comes down like a
glorious cherub, and lights on her bosom, with
this message from God, 'I have heard thy prayers,
and seen thy tears'; so with a handkerchief of
comfort dries her cheeks, and tells her that she
is accepted in Jesus Christ.

In dust and ashes.—I have but one stair more,
down from both text and pulpit; and it is a very
low one—'dust and ashes.'

An adorned body is not the vehicle of a
humbled soul. Job, before his affliction, was not
poor. Doubtless he had his wardrobe, his change
and choice of garments. Yet now, how doth his

humbled soul contemn them, as if he threw away
his vesture, saying, I have worn thee for pomp,
given countenance to a silken case ; I quite mis-
took thy nature ; get thee from me, I am weary
of thy service ; thou hast made me honourable
with men, thou canst get me no estimation before
the Lord.   Repentance gives a farewell not only
to wonted delights, but even to natural refreshings.
Job lies not on a bed of roses and violets, as did
the Sybarites ; nor on a couch beautified with the
tapestry of Egypt ; but on a bed of ashes.
Sackcloth is his apparel ; dust and ashes the lace
and embroidery of it.   Thus Nineveh's king, upon
that fearful sentence, 'rose from his throne, laid
his robe from him, covered himself with sackcloth,
and sat in ashes,' Jonah iii. 6.   Oh, what an
alteration can repentance make !   From a king
of the earth to a worm of the earth ; from a
footcloth to sackcloth ; from a throne to a dunghill ; from sitting in state to lying in ashes !
Whom all the reverence of the world attended on,
to whom the head was uncovered, the knee bowed,
the body prostrated ; who had as many salutations
as the firmament stars,—God save the king !—he
throws away crown, sceptre, majesty, and all, and
sits in ashes.   How many doth the golden cup of
honour make drunk, and drive from all sense of
mortality !   Riches and heart's ease are such

usual intoxications to the souls of men, that it is rare to find any of them so low as dust and ashes.

Dust, as the remembrance of his original; ashes, as the representation of his end. Dust, that was the mother; ashes, that shall be the daughter of our bodies.

Dust, the matter of our substance, the house of our souls, the original grains whereof we were made, the top of all our kindred. The glory of the strongest man, the beauty of the fairest woman, all is but dust. Dust, the only compounder of differences, the absolver of all distinctions. Who can say which was the client, which the lawyer; which the borrower, which the lender; which the captive, which the conqueror, when they all lie together in blended dust?

Dust; not marble nor porphyry, gold nor precious stone, was the matter of our bodies, but earth, and the fractions of the earth, dust. Dust, the sport of the wind, the very slave of the besom. This is the pit from whence we are digged, and this is the pit to which we shall be resolved. 'Dust thou art, and to dust thou shalt return again,' Gen. iii. 18. They that sit in the dust, and feel their own materials about them, may well renounce the ornaments of pride, the gulf of avarice, the foolish lusts of concupiscence. Let the covetous think, What do I scrape for? a little golden dust;

the ambitious, What do I aspire for? a little honourable dust; the libidinous, What do I languish for? a little animated dust, blown away with the breath of God's displeasure.

Oh, how goodly this building of man appears when it is clothed with beauty and honour! A face full of majesty, the throne of comeliness, wherein the whiteness of the lily contends with the sanguine of the rose; an active hand, an erected countenance, an eye sparkling out lustre, a smooth complexion, arising from an excellent temperature and composition; whereas other creatures, by reason of their cold and gross humours, are grown over, beasts with hair, fowls with feathers, fishes with scales. Oh, what a workman was this, that could raise such a fabric out of the earth, and lay such orient colours upon dust! Yet all is but dust, walking, talking, breathing dust; all this beauty but the effect of a well-concocted food, and life itself but a walk from dust to dust. Yea, and this man, or that woman, is never so beautiful as when they sit weeping for their sins in the dust: as Mary Magdalene was then fairest when she kneeled in the dust, bathing the feet of Christ with her tears, and wiping them with her hairs; like heaven, fair sight-ward to us that are without, but more fair to them that are within.

THE SINNER'S MOURNING-HABIT

An old man is said to give Alexander a little jewel, and told him that it had this virtue, so long as he kept it bright, it would outvalue the most fine gold or precious stone in the world ; but if it once took dust it would not be worth a feather. What meant the sage, but to give the monarch an emblem of his own body, which, being animated with a soul, commanded the world ; but once fallen to dust, it would be worth nothing, 'for a living dog is better than a dead lion,' Eccles. ix. 4.

I conclude ; I call you not to casting dust on your heads or sitting in ashes, but to that sorrow and compunction of soul whereof the other was but an external symbol or testimony. Let us rend our hearts and spare our garments, humble our souls without afflicting our bodies, Isa. lviii. 5. It is not a corpse wrapped in dust and ashes, but a contrite heart, which the Lord will not despise, Ps. li. 17. Let us repent our sins and amend our lives ; so God will pardon us by the merits, save us by the mercies, and crown us with the glories of Jesus Christ.

THE COSMOPOLITE;

OR,

WORLD'S FAVOURITE

*But God said unto him, Thou fool, this night thy
soul shall be required of thee: then whose
shall those things be, which thou hast provided?*—Luke xii. 20.

THIS is the covetous man's scripture; and
both (like an unflattering glass) presents his
present condition, what he is, and (like an unflattering book) premonstrates his future state,
what he shall be.

First, we have the rich man prospering in his
wealth; secondly, we have him caring what to do.
He had so much gain, so much grain, that his
rooms could not answer the capacity of his heart.
'What shall I do, because I have no room where
to bestow my fruits?' Care is the inseparable
companion of abundance. They to whom is given
most wealth are most given to carking, sharking,
and solicitous thoughtfulness. Those hearts whom
the world hath done most to satisfy, are least of
all satisfied. Thirdly, we have his resolution.

'This will I do.' What? 'I will pull down my barns, and build greater ; and there will I bestow all my fruits and my goods.' He thinks of no room in the bowels of the poor ; which the Lord hath proposed to him a fit receptacle of his superfluity. He minds not to build an hospital, or to repair a church ; either to the worship of Christ, or education of orphans, or consolations of distressed souls ; but only respects his barn and his barley. The want of room troubles him ; his harvest was so great, that he is crop-sick. The stomach of his barn is too little to hold that surfeit of corn he intends it ; and therefore in anger he will pull it down, and make it answerable to his own desires. This he takes as granted, and upon the new building of his barn he builds his rest : ver. 19, 'Then I will say to my soul, Soul, thou hast much goods laid up for many years ; take thine ease, eat, drink, and be merry.' He dreams his belly full, and now his pipes go ; he sings *requiem*, and lullabies his spirit in the cradle of his barn. This sweet news he whispers to his soul. Though he had wearied his body with incessant toils, and made it a galley-slave to his imperious affection ; yet his soul had been especially disquieted, and therefore he promiseth his soul some ease. In this indulgent promise, there is a preface and a solace :—

1. The preface assures his soul 'much goods,' and 'many years.' He knew that a scant and sparing proffer would not satisfy his boundless desires; there must be show of an abundant impletion. It is not enough to have an ample rock or distaff of wealth, unless a longeval time be afforded to spin it out. Philoxenus's wish coupled with his pleasant viands a long throat, crane-like, to prolong his delight: for shortness doth somewhat abate sweetness. *Rex horæ*, a king of one hour, can scarce warm his throne; it keeps a Christmas-lord flat, that he knows his end. If this man had been his own lord, how excellent an estate would he have assured himself! His farm should have been so large, and his lease so long, that I doubt whether Adam in paradise had a greater lordship, or Methusalem a longer life. The last of his desires is of the longest size: give him much goods and much time, abundance of joys and abundance of days, and you hit or fit the length of his foot.

2. The solace is a dance of four paces: 'Take thine ease, eat, drink, and be merry.' The full belly loves an easy-chair; he must needs join with his laborious surfeits the vacation of sleep. He hath taken great pains to bring death upon him; and now standing at his door, it hears him talk of *ease*. He promiseth himself that which he travails

to destroy, life; and even now ends what he threatens to begin. So worldlings weary and wear out their lives to hoard wealth; and when wealth comes, and health goes, they would give all for life. O fools! in continual quest of riches, to hunt themselves out of breath, and then be glad to restore all at once for recovery. The next pace is, *Eat*: his bones must not only be pleased, but his belly. It is somewhat yet that this man resolves at last no more to pinch his guts; therefore what before he was in their debt, he will pay them with the usury of surfeits. He purposeth to make himself of a thin starveling, a fat epicure; and so to translate *parcum* into *porcum*. The third pace is, *Drink*: where gluttony is bid welcome, there is no shutting out of drunkenness. You shall not take a Nabal, but he plies his goblet as well as his trencher. And this is a ready course to retire himself from his former vexation, to drown his cares in wine. The last pace is a levalto, *Be merry*: when he hath got junkets in his belly, and wines in his brain, what should he do but leap, dance, revel, be merry, be mad! After feasting must follow jesting. Here be all the four passages: he sleeps care away, he eats care away, he drinks care away, and now he sings care away. His pipes be full, and they must needs squeak, though the name of the good, yea, the name of God, be dishonoured. But to such a mad-merry scoffer might well be applied that verse which was sounded in the ear of a great rhymer dying. Leave playing, and fall to praying: it is but sorry jesting with death. Thus his dance was like Sardanapalus's : *Ede, bibe, lude,*—Eat, drink, and be merry ; but there is one thing mars all his sport, the bringing of his soul to judgment. He promiseth a merry life, and a long life ; but death says nay to both. He gratifies his soul, and ratifies his state ; but cozens himself in all. It may be said of him, as King John of the fat stag dying : ' See how easily he hath lived, yet he never heard mass.' This was the sweet, but the sour follows. He rejoiceth with the world, but must not live in glory with Christ.

But now God will be heard: 'He said'; he spoke home ; a word and a blow. He will be understood, though not stood under. This is such a sermon as shall not pass without consideration. So he preached to Pharaoh by frogs, flies, locusts, murrain, darkness ; but when neither by Moses's vocal, nor by these actual lectures he would be melted, the last sermon is a Red Sea, that drowns him and his army. The tree is bared, manured, watered, spared in expectancy of fruits ; but when none comes, the last sermon is the axe : it must be 'hewn down and cast into the fire,' Matt. iii. 10.

This kind of argument is unanswerable, and cannot be evaded. When 'God gives the word, innumerable are the preachers'; if the lower voices will not be heard, death shall be feared. God knocks long by his prophets, yea, 'stands at the door' himself, Rev. iii. 20; we will not open. But when this preacher comes, he opens the door himself, and will not be denied entrance. The rich man must hear this sermon; there is no remedy. 'But God said—Thou fool.'

What! if this had come from a poor tenant's mouth, it had been held a petty kind of blasphemy. Is the rich man only held the wise man at all parts; and doth God change his title with such a contradiction? Is the world's gold become dross? the rich idol a fool? It is even a maxim in common acceptation, 'He is wise that is rich.' Rich and wise are convertible terms, imagined to signify one thing. When the rich man speaks, all the people give bareheaded silence and attention.

In the church surely religion should have the strongest force; yet riches thrusts in her head even under religion's arm, and speaks her mind. Money once brought the greatest preacher of the gospel, even the author of the gospel, Christ himself, to be judged before an earthly tribunal.

In the courts of justice, law should rule; yet

169

often money overrules law and court too. It is a lamentable complaint in the prophecy of Isaiah, 'Judgment is turned away backward, and justice standeth afar off: for truth is fallen in the street, and equity cannot enter,' Isa. lix. 14.

In the wars valour bears a great stroke, yet not so great as money. That Macedonian monarch was wont to say he would never fear to surprise that city whose gates were wide enough for an ass laden with gold to enter. How many forts, castles, cities, kingdoms hath that blown up before ever gunpowder was invented. I need name no more. What quality bears up so brave a head but money gives it the checkmate! It answereth all things, saith Solomon.

We see the patient, let us come now to the *passion*, or suffering. This is the point of war, which my text sounds like a trumpet, against all worldlings : 'This night shall thy soul be required of thee.'

What? The 'soul,' thy soul : not thy barns, nor thy crop ; neither the continent, nor content ; not thy goods, which thou holdest dear, nor thy body, which thou prizest dearer, but thy soul, which should be to thee dearest of all. Imagine the whole convex of heaven for thy barn, (and that were one large enough,) and all the riches of the world thy grain, (and that were crop sufficient,) yet put all these into one balance, and thy soul into the other, and thy soul outweighs, outvalues the world. 'What is the whole world worth to him that loseth his soul?' The soul is of a precious nature.

One in substance, like the sun, yet of diverse operations. It is confined in the body, not refined by the body, but is often most active when her jailor is most dull. She is a careful housewife, disposing all well at home; conserving all forms, and mustering them to her own serviceable use. The senses discern the outside, the circumstance, the husk of things; she the inside, the virtue, the marrow: resolving effects into causes; compounding, comparing, contemplating things in their highest sublimity. Fire turns coals into fire; the body concocts meat into blood; but the soul converts body into spirits, reducing their purest forms within her dimensive lines. In man's composition there is a shadow of the Trinity. For to make up one man there is an elementary body, a divine soul, and a firmamental spirit. Here is the difference: in God there are three persons in one essence, in us three essences in one person. So in the soul there is a trinity of powers, vegetable, sensitive, rational: the former would only *be*; the second be, and *be well*; the third be, be well, and be *for ever* well. O excellent nature, in whose cabinet ten thousand forms may sit at once; which gives agitation to the body, without whom it would fall down a dead and inanimate lump of clay! This soul shall be required.

'Thy soul,' which understands what delight is, and conceives a tickling pleasure in these covetous desires. But to satisfy thy soul, thou wouldst not be so greedy of abundance; for a little serves the body. If it have food to sustain it, garments to hide it, harbour to shelter it, liberty to refresh it, it is contented. And satiety of these things doth not comfort, but confound it. Too much meat surfeits the body, too much apparel wearies it, too much wine drowns it; only *quod convenit, conservat*. It is, then, the soul that requires this plenitude, and therefore from this plenitude shall the soul be required.

'Thy soul,' which is not made of a perishing nature, as the body, but of an everlasting substance; and hath by the eternity thereof a capableness of more joy or more sorrow: it must be ever in heaven or ever in hell. This night must this soul receive her doom; 'thy soul shall be required.'

That soul which shall be the body's perpetual companion, saving a short divorce by the hand of death in the grave; but afterwards ordained to an everlasting reunion. Whereas all worldly goods, being once broken off by death, can never again be recovered. The soul shall return to the body, but riches to neither ; and this soul must be required.

This is a loss, a cross beyond all that the worldling's imagination can give being to. How differ the wicked's thoughts dying from their thoughts living ! In the days of their peace they forget to get for the soul any good. Either it must rest itself on these inferior props, or despair of refuge. The eye is not scanted of lustful objects, the ear of melodious sounds, the palate of well-relished viands : but the soul's eye is not fastened on heaven, nor her ears on the word of God ; her taste savours not the bread of life ; she is neither brought to touch nor to smell on Christ's vesture. *Animas habent, quasi inanimata vivunt :* regarding their flesh as that pampered Roman did his, and their souls as he esteemed his horse ; who being a spruce, neat, and fat epicure, and riding on a lean, scraggy jade, was asked by the censors the reason. His answer was, I look to myself, but my man to my horse. So these worldlings look to their bodies, let who will take care of their souls.

But when this night comes, with what a price would they purchase again their souls, so mortgaged to the devil for a little vanity ! With what studious and artificial cost is the body adorned, whiles the beggarly soul lies in tattered rags! The flesh is pleased with the purest flour of the wheat, and reddest blood of the grape; the soul is famished. The body is allowed liberty, even to licentiousness; the soul is under Satan's lock and key, shackled with the fetters of ignorance and impiety. At this night's terror, to what bondage, hunger, cold, calamity, would they not subject their bodies, to free their souls out of that friendless and endless prison! Why cannot men think of this before it be too late? It will sound harshly in thine ear, O thou riotous or avarous worldling, when this passing-bell rings, 'Thy soul shall be required!' If the prince should confiscate thy goods, which thou lovest so dearly, this news would strike cold to thy heart; but here thy soul is confiscate. Thou hast offended, O miserable cosmopolite, against thy great Sovereign's law, crown, and majesty; now all thou hast is confiscate—thy goods, thy body, thy soul. Thou, whose whole desires were set to scrape all together, shalt now find all scattered asunder; thy close congestion meets with a wide dispersion. This sudden call is fearful: 'This night shall thy soul be required.' Yet before I part from this point, let me give you two notes :—

First, There is mercy in God that it is this

night; not this *hour*, not this *moment*. *Hac nocte* was sudden, but *hoc momento* had been more sudden ; and that this larger exhibition of time is allowed was God's mere mercy against the worldling's merit. He that spared Nineveh many forties of years will yet allow her forty days, Jonah iii. 4. He that forbore this wretch many days, receiving no fruit worth his expectation, will yet add a few hours. God, in the midst of justice, remembers mercy : much time he had received and abused, yet he shall have a little more. When the Lord's hand is lifted up to strike him, yet he gives him some *lucida intervalla monitionis,*— warning before he lets it down. But let not the worldling presume on this ; sometimes not an hour, not a minute is granted. Sword, palsy, apoplexy, imposthume, make quick despatch, and there is no space given to cry for mercy. Conversion at the eleventh hour is a wonder, at the twelfth a miracle. All thieves do not go from the gallows to glory because one did, no more than all asses speak because God opened the mouth of one. Flatter not thyself with hope of time. Man's life is compared to a day.

This day to some may be distinguished into twelve hours. The first gives us nativity : even in this hour there is sin ; an original pravity, indisposition to good, proneness to evil. Secondly,

infancy : God now protects the cradle. Thirdly,
childhood : and now we learn to speak and to
swear together ; the sap of iniquity begins to put
out. Fourthly, tender age : wherein toys and
gauds fill up our scene. Fifthly, youth : this is a
madding, a gadding time. 'Remember not the
sins' of this time, prays David, Ps. xxv. 7 ; their
'remembrance is bitter,' says Job, chap. xiii. 26.
Sixthly, our high noon : God, that could not be
heard before for the loud noise of vanity, now looks
for audience.

But here is his end, you must read him no
further : 'He whom you have seen this day, you
shall see him again no more for ever,' Exod. xiv.
13. 'Whose shall these things be,' O worldling ?
Were thy grounds as Eden, and thy house like
the court of Jehoiakim, yet 'dost thou think to
reign, because thou closest thyself in cedar ?'
Jer. xxii. 15. No ; thy end is come ; 'whose
shall these things be ?'

It were something yet if thy children might
enjoy these riches. But there is a man that 'hath
no child, yet is there no end of his labour ; neither
is his eye satisfied with wealth ; and he saith not,
'For whom do I travail, and bereave my soul of
this good ?' Eccles. iv. 8. The prodigal would be
his own heir and executor ; but this covetous man
bequeaths neither legacy to himself, nor to any

known inheritor. The other desires to see an end of all his substance; this man to see only the beginning. He hunts the world full cry, yet hath no purpose to overtake it; he lives behind his wealth, as the other lives beyond it. But suppose he hath children, and then though he famish himself to feed them fat; though he be damned, yet if his son be made a gentleman, there is some satisfaction. But this *Cujus erunt* is a scattering word, and of great uncertainty. 'Whose shall they be?' Perhaps not thy children's. They say, 'Happy is that son whose father goes to the devil,' but thou mayest go to the devil, and yet not make thy son happy. For men make heritages, but God makes heirs. He will wash away the unholy seed, and cut off the generation of the wicked. Solomon had a thousand wives and concubines, and consequently many children; yet at last he wants one of his 'seed to sit upon the throne of David, or to bear rule in Judah.' It often so falls out, that to a man exceeding wealthy is denied a successor of his own loins. Let him have children, he is not sure those children shall possess his riches. 'But those riches perish by evil travail; and he begetteth a son, and there is nothing in his hand,' Eccles. v. 14. A scatterer succeeds a gatherer; the father loved the world too well, and the son cares not for it. The sire was all for the rake, and the son is all for the pitchfork. So, 'whose shall all these be?' Even his that will one day pity the poor.

But perhaps if thou hast no children thou hast a brother. Thou bequeathest it to thy brother, but God disposeth it to his children. But thou hast no brother, yet thou hast kindred and friends; and to help thy cousins to wealth, thou wilt cozen thy own soul! Alas! it is a mystery of knowledge to discern friends. 'Wealth maketh many friends,' Prov. xix. 4; they are friends to the wealth, not to the wealthy.

Worldly friends are but like hot water, that when cold weather comes, are soonest frozen. Like cuckoos, all summer they will sing a scurvy note to thee, but they are gone in July at furthest: sure enough before the fall. They flatter a rich man, as we feed beasts, till he be fat, and then feed on him. A true friend reproves thee erring, though perhaps not suddenly. Iron is first heated, then beaten: first let him be heated with due and deserved praise for his good, then cool and work him with reprehension for his evil; as nurses, when their children are fallen, first take them up, and speak them fair, and chide or correct them afterwards. These friends love not thy soul's good, but thy body's goods; let them not carry away thy heart from Christ.

All these particulars surveyed give the covetous cosmopolite three brands. He is branded in his soul, in his riches, in his good name. In his soul: 'Thy soul shall be fetched away.' In his riches: 'Whose shall these things be which thou hast provided?' In his name: 'Thou fool.' Whereupon we may justly infer this conclusion as the sum of all: that abundant wealth can bring no good either to soul, body, or name. Man is said to have three lives: spiritual, corporal, and civil, as the lawyers call it—the life of his good name. Neither to this, nor to the life of his soul or body, can multitude of riches confer any good. This text shall prove it in all the particulars :—

1. To the *soul* can opulency procure no benefit. All Christians know that good for the soul is the passion and merits of Christ: faith to apprehend these; repentance to mortify sins; sanctification to give us celestial lives; and salvation to glorify our persons. But can any of these be bought with money? 'Thou and thy money perish together, that thinkest the gifts of God may be purchased with money,' Acts viii. 20. God will not barter away his graces (as the Indians their gold) for thy gauds and rattles. He will not take the mortgage of a lordship for the debt thou owest him. The smoke of thy sacrifice smells never the sweeter because thou art clothed in silks, or canst sit down

to tell thy Michaelmas thousands. Thy adulteries cannot be commuted for in heaven, nor thy usuries be answered by a fine before the tribunal of the Highest. Thou mayest as soon and easily mount up to heaven with wings of lead as by feathers of wealth. Indeed, they can do a man as much good in distress of conscience, as to have his head bound with a wet cloth in a cold morning can cure the headache. If wealth could keep a man from hell, how few rich men would be damned! But he is not *sanctior qui ditior*; nor is salvation vendible to a full purse. The doctrine of Rome may affirm it; but the decree of God will not afford it. This cosmopolite had barns and bars, but these cannot hedge in his soul; that is 'required.'

2. To the *body* perhaps there is some more expectation of good, but no more success. Thou art anguished : will thy wealth purchase health? Sleep is denied thy senses, and after many changed sides and places, thou canst find no rest : go now, empty thy coffers, and try what slumber the charms and chimes of gold can ring thee. Thy stomach loathes meat : all thy riches are not sufficient sauce to get thee an appetite. Couldst thou drink Cleopatra's draught, it will not ease thy headache. The physician will take thy money, and give thee physic ; but what physic will give thee infallible health?

But the rich man hath a fire, when the poor sits cold; the rich a harbour, attendance, and delicate provision, when the poor wants both house and home, meat and money, garments and company. For though riches gather many friends, 'the poor is separated from his neighbours,' Prov. xix. 4. No part of my sermon hath denied but the competency of these earthly things is a blessing; neither dare I infer that the want of these is a curse; for the best have wanted them, not the Saviour of men himself excepted. But what is this to abundance? Is not he as warm that goes in russet as another that rustles and ruffles in his silks? Hath not the poor labourer as sound a sleep on his flock-bed or pad of straw as the epicure on his down-bed, with his rich curtains and coverings? Doth not quiet lie oftener in cottages than in glorious manors? 'The sleep of a labouring man is sweet, whether he eat little or much; but the abundance of the rich will not suffer him to sleep.'

3. The *name* perhaps hath some hope of luxurious share in this abundance, and thinks to be swelled into a *Colossus*, over-straddling the world. There is more hope of a great name than of good content. And now for the name; what is the event? What is credit, or how may we define a good name? Is it to have a pageant

of cringes and faces acted to a taffety jacket? To be
followed by a world of hang-byes, and hooted at
by the reeling multitude, like a bird of paradise,
stuck full of pied feathers? To have poor men
crouch to him, as little dogs use to a great mastiff?
Is this a good name? Is this credit? Indeed
these things may give him a great sound, but the
bell is hollow. He may think himself the better ;
but no wise man, no good man doth ; and the
fame that is derived from fools is infamy.

That which I take to be a good name is this :
to be well esteemed of in Christian hearts ; to find
reverence in good men's souls. It is a good thing
to be praised, but it is a better to be praiseworthy.
It is well that good men commend thee in their
consciences, but it is better when thy good conscience can commend thee in itself. Happy is
he whose 'own heart doth not condemn him,'
1 John iii. 21. This credit wealth cannot procure,
but grace ; not goods, but goodness. The poorest
man serving God with a faithful heart, finds this
approbation in sanctified affections, when golden
asses go without it. I confess, many rich men
have had this credit, but they will never thank
their riches for it. Their greatness never helped
them to this name, but their goodness. They
have honoured the Lord, and those the Lord
hath promised that he will honour.

To conclude : it may be yet objected, that though much wealth can procure to soul, body or name, no good ; yet it may be an antidote to prevent some evil. What evil then can riches either prevent or remove from man?

1. Not from the soul ; all evil to this is either of sin or of punishment for sin. What vice is evacuated by riches? Is the wealthy man humbled by his abundance? Wealth is no charm to conjure away the devil ; such an amulet and the Pope's holy-water are both of a force. Inward vexations forbear not their stings in awe of riches. An evil conscience dares perplex a Saul in his throne, and a Judas with his purse full of money. Can a silken sleeve keep a broken arm from aching? Then may full barns keep an evil conscience from vexing.

2. Nor from the body can riches remove any plague. The lightning from heaven may consume us, though we be clad in gold ; the vapours of earth choke us, though perfumes are still in our nostrils ; and poison burst us, though we have the most virtual antidotes. What judgment is the poor subject to, from which the rich is exempted? Their feet do as soon stumble, and their bones are as quickly broken. Consumptions, fevers, gouts, dropsies, pleurisies, palsies, surfeits, are household guests in rich men's families, and but

mere strangers in cottages. They are the effects of superfluous fare and idleness; and keep their ordinary at rich men's tables. Anguish lies oftener on a down-bed than on a pallet; diseases wait upon luxury as close as luxury upon wealth. These frogs dare leap into King Pharaoh's chamber, and forbear not the most sumptuous palace. But money can buy medicines: yet, what sick man would not wish that he had no money, on condition that he had no malady! Labour and moderate diet are the poor man's friends, and preserve him from the acquaintance of Master Doctor, or the surfeited bills of his apothecary. Though our worldling here promiseth out of his abundance, meat, drink, and mirth; yet his body grows sick, and his soul sad: he was before careless, and he is now cureless; all his wealth cannot retain his health, when God will take it away.

3. But what shall we say to the estate? Evils to that are poverty, hunger, thirst, weariness, servility. We hope wealth can stop the invasion of these miseries. Nothing less: it rather mounts a man, as a wrestler does his combatant, that it may give him the greater fall. Riches are but a shield of wax against a sword of power. The larger state, the fairest mark for misfortune to shoot at. Eagles catch not after flies; nor will

the Hercules of ambition lift up his club but against these giants. There is not in poverty that matter for a great man's covetous fire to work upon. If Naboth had had no vineyard to prejudice the command of Ahab's lordship, he had saved both his peace and life. Violent winds blow through a hollow willow, or over a poor shrub, and let them stand, whiles they rend a-pieces oaks and great cedars, that oppose their great bodies to the furious blasts. The tempests of oppressing power meddle not with the contemptible quiet of poor labourers, but shake up rich men by the very roots ; that their blasted fortunes may be fit timber for their own building. Who stands so like an eyesore in the tyrannous sight of ambition as the wealthy? Imprisonment, restraint, banishment, confiscation, fining, and confining are greatness's intelligencers ; instruments and stairs to climb up by into rich men's possessions.

I end, then, as Paul concludes his counsel to rich men : 'Lay up for yourselves a good foundation against the time to come, that you may lay hold on eternal life,' 1 Tim. vi. 19.

THE TWO SONS;

OR,

THE DISSOLUTE CONFERRED WITH THE HYPOCRITE

But what think you? A certain man had two sons; and he came to the first, and said, Son, go work to-day in my vineyard. He answered and said, I will not: but afterward he repented, and went. And he came to the second, and said likewise. And he answered and said, I go, sir: but he went not.— Matt. xxi. 28—30.

THE priests and elders quarrel with our Saviour, ver. 23, about his authority. Christ requites them, by demanding their opinion concerning the baptism of John. Here is question against question: the Jews appose Jesus, Jesus apposeth the Jews. Neither of them doth answer the other: the elders could and durst not, our Saviour could and would not. Indeed, Christ's very question was a sufficient answer and resolution of their demand; their own consciences bearing against them invincible witness, that as John's baptism, so our Saviour's authority, was immediately derived from heaven.

Well, the former question would not be answered: now Christ puts another to them; if with any better success. The other they understand, but dare not answer; this they dare answer, but not understand, lest they should conclude themselves those hypocritical sons that say they will, and do not, against whom heavengate is so fast shut that publicans and harlots shall first be admitted. 'But what think you?' If you dare not open your lips, I appeal to your hearts; your tongues may be kept silent, your consciences cannot be insensible. I come to your thoughts: 'What think you?'

There is an induction, 'A certain man had two sons.' A production, which consists of a double charge, a double answer, a double event:—
1. Here is the father's charge to his eldest son: 'Son, go work to-day in my vineyard.' 2. His answer is negative: 'I will not.' 3. His obedience was affirmative: 'He repented and went.' So, 1. The father's command to his younger son was the same. 2. His answer is affirmative: 'I go, sir.' 3. The event was negative: 'He went not.' You hear the propositions; assume to yourselves, and the conclusion will tell you whether of these sons you are.

We will begin with the father's charge to his

eldest son: 'Son, go and work to-day in my vine-yard.' God doth lay the imposition of labour upon his sons. The charge of working in the vineyard belongs to a Christian, not only as he is a servant, but even as he is a son to God. Whether we be friends or sons, stands in this if we be servants. If thou be my son, work in my vine-yard. The son is not exempted from doing his father's business.

Without this, vain is the ostentation of other titles. Many and excellent are the attributions which the Scripture giveth us; as friends, children, heirs, &c. Most men arrogate these, as the sweet privileges of ease, honour, benefit. They imagine that facility, a soft and gentle life, is hence warranted: that it is glory enough to be God's friend or son. Saul will be God's friend, if it be but for his kingdom. The Jews title themselves God's sons, that they may be his heirs. Whiles the door of adoption is thought to stand open in the gospel, infinite flock in thither; not for love, but gain. Again, these stand most in affection; and, dwelling inwardly, may with the more ease be dissembled. The profession of many is like the mountebank's trunk, which his host seeing fairly bound with a gaudy cover, and weighty in poise, had his trust deceived with the rubbish and stones within.

Only service hath neither ease nor concealment allotted it, because it consists in a visible action. Many say they are God's friends, but they will do nothing for him. Let a distressed member of their Saviour pass by them, with never so hearty beseechings and pitiful complaints, they are dry nurses; not a drop of milk comes from them. Call you these God's friends? Let profane swaggerers blaspheme God's sacred name; where is their controlment? They cannot endure a serpent, yet give close society to a blasphemer; whereas this wretch is worse than anything. This caitiff, like a mad dog, flies in his master's face that keeps him. Whoso can endure this, and not have their blood rise, and their very souls moved, are no friends to God. It is a poor part of friendship to stand silent by whiles a friend's good name is traduced. Such a man is possessed with a dumb devil. If men were God's friends, they would frequent God's house: there is little friendship to God where there is no respect of his presence, nor affection to his company. Our Saviour throughly decides this: 'Ye are my friends, if ye do whatsoever I command you,' John xv. 14. There is no friendship where no obedience.

Casting over this whole reckoning, we find the sum this: God hath few friends, kindred, sons, because he hath few servants. How many have promised good hopes to themselves, and not unlikely to us, that they were God's children, against whom the gate of heaven hath been shut for want of actual service! Let men never plead acquaintance, familiarity, sonship, when God tries them, as this son, what they will do for him, and they refuse to work in his vineyard. It must be the word, written on the scutcheon of every Christian soldier—I SERVE. And yet some, as they presume themselves to be God's sons, so they assume to be his servants; and have evidence to neither of these claims. They will be held God's servants, yet never did good char in his house. They may, not unfitly, be compared to retainers; for as great men's retainers lightly visit their lord once by the year, and that at Christmas, and then rather for good cheer than love: so these deal with God; come to his table at Easter, and there they will feast with him, that the world may take notice they belong to him; which done, they bid him farewell till the next year.

So that if God have indented with us to save us as sons, we must indent with him to serve him as servants. 'The heir, so long as he is a child, differeth nothing from a servant, though he be lord of all,' Gal. iv. 1. It hath pleased God to adopt us co-heirs with his blessed Son to an immortal inheritance; yet so long as we live on earth, we are but in our minority, and therefore differ not from servants. Though he gives us the vineyard, yet we must first work in it.

But the father here sets his eldest son to work. If any business be to be done, our custom is to impose all on the younger, and favour the elder. It is enough for him to see fashions abroad. This indulgence too often turns to ruin; for long unrestrained wantonness, and unchidden pride, teacheth him at last, though his now dead father left him much lands, to carry them all up in his purse to London; whence he lightly brings nothing down, but a few new-fangled rags, or perhaps a church on his back, and the bells at his heels; as one said of the church-robber's heir with jingling spurs. Too many run to such riot in the April of their years, that they soon bring December on their houses, and sell their patrimony to some supplanter for pottage. They so toss and bandy their estates, from vanity to vanity, from madness to madness, till at last they fall into the usurer's hazard. And once lying at the extortioner's mercy by forfeit, it is as surely damned as the extortioner himself will be when he lies at the mercy of the devil. The mind having once caught the trick of running out, is hardly banked in. He that is used to a torch scorns to go with a candle. It is a good course:

let them work in the vineyard before they have it,
they will keep it the better when they have it.
But some fathers are so dotingly kind, that they
put themselves out of their estates to fasten them
on their eldest son. Alas, poor men! how few of
them ever die without cursing the time when they
made themselves slaves to their cradles!

Every one thinks himself God's son : then hear
his voice, 'Go, my son.' You have all your vine-
yards to go to. Magistrates, go to the bench, to
execute judgment and justice; ministers, go to
the temple, to preach, to pray, to do the work of
evangelists; people, go to your callings, that you
may eat the labours of your own hands. Eye to
thy seeing, ear to thy hearing, foot to thy walking,
hand to thy working; Peter to thy nets, Paul to
thy tents; every man to his profession, according
to that station wherein God hath disposed us.

The *limitation* of time instructs you : 'to-day.'
We need not grudge God our labour; it is but a
day wherein we are enjoined to work : Ps. civ. 23,
' Man goeth forth to his work, and to his labour
until the evening'; not only that little part of
time, the artificial day, as they call it, but even
his whole natural day of life, till his sun set. Time
is precious; and howsoever our pride and lusts
think it, God so highly prizeth it, that he will
punish the loss of a short time with a revenge

beyond all times : the misspense of a temporal
day with an eternal night. Every hour hath
wings, and there is no moment passing from us
but it flies up to the Maker of time, and bears
him true tidings how we have used it. There is
no usury tolerable but of two things, grace and
time ; and it is only blessed wealth that is gotten
by improving them to the best. We brought with
us into the world sin enough to repent of all our
short day. There is no minute flies over our
heads without new addition to our sins, and therefore brings new reason for our sorrows. We
little think that every moment we misspend is a
record against us in heaven, or that every idle
hour is entered into God's registry, and stands
there in capital letters till our repentant tears
wash it out. The Ancient of days sees us fool
away our time, as if we had eternity before us.
Harlots, taverns, theatres, markets of vanity, take
up whole weeks, months, years ; and we are old
ere we consider ourselves mortal. Not so many
sands are left in the glass as a sparrow can take
in her bill, before we think we have lost much
time, or perceive we have no more to lose.
Nothing is of that nature that life is ; for it loseth
by getting, diminisheth by increasing, and every
day that is added to it is so much by a day taken
from it. That very night which thou last sleptest

hath by a night shortened thy life. So insensibly runs away our time, though we entreat it never so earnestly to slacken the pace. How fond are they that invent for it pastimes!

Distinguish our day into a morning, noon, and evening. Our youth, which is our morning, we most usually (not usefully) spend in toys and vanities: as if it were not a fault in a young man to wantonise, dance, drink, swear, swagger, revel. Our old age, which is our afternoon, for the most part is spent in caring, trouble, and anxiety for this world; our distrustful hearts still asking, How shall we do when we are old? yet being so old already, that there is no possible good means of spending what we have. So that here remains nothing but the noon of our day. As Epaminondas aptly said, Young men should be saluted with Good-morrow, or welcome into the world; old men with Good-night, because they are taking their leaves of the world; only men of middle age with Good-day. This mid-day is only left for the vineyard, and how much of it spend we in working there?

The time of our working is not only confined, but the place defined,—'in my vineyard.' Not in the wilderness of the world, nor in the labyrinth of lusts, nor in the orchard of vain delights, nor in the field of covetousness, nor in the house of

security, much less in the chamber of wantonness,
or tavern of drunkenness, or theatre of lewdness ;
but in my vineyard. We must not only be doing,
but be doing what we ought. True obedience is
a readiness to do as we are bidden.

God scorns that the world or the flesh should
set down rules how he will be served. He never
made the devil his steward, to appoint his sons to
their task. The king having made positive laws
and decrees whereby he will govern either his
public or private house, his kingdom or family,
disdains that a groom should contradict and annul
those, to dignify and advance other of his own
fiction. Paul durst not 'confer with flesh and
blood,' Gal. i. 16, when God had imposed on him
an office. That obedience of Abraham, which
was so highly praised, was punctually dependent
on God's command. He is a sorry servant that,
on the first bidding, runs away without his errand.
There is a generation of men that are too
laborious : curious statesmen in foreign commonwealths, busy bishops in others' dioceses, scalding
their lips in their neighbour's pottage. This is an
ambitious age of meddlers ; there are almost as
many minds as men, sects as cities, gospels as
gossips : as if they laboured the reducing of the
old chaos and first informity of things again. So
the foxes do without labour make spoil of the

grapes ; and these endeavours do not help, but hurt the vineyard. Painfulness is not only required, but profitableness. Otherwise, as it is said of the schoolmen, they may *magno conatu nihil agere*,—take great pains to no purpose. There is no action but hath his labour ; and the proportion of it differs, and is made less or more according to the will of the agent. Whatsoever difficulty there is, ariseth rather from the doer than from the work. What we do willingly, seems easy. Some can follow their dogs a whole day in the field with delight, upon whom, if authority should impose the measuring so many paces, how often would they complain of weariness ! Let good-fellows sit in a tavern from sun to sun, and they think the day very short, confessing (though insensible of the loss) that time is a light-heeled runner. Bind them to the church for two hours, and you put an ache into their bones, the seats be too hard : now time is held a cripple, and many a weary look is cast up to the glass. It is a man's mind that makes any work pleasant or troublesome.

The charge is ended : the next point objected to our consideration is the son's answer, ' I will not.'

We have not been so long about the charge, but the son is as short in his answer : ' I will not.'

A very strange speech of a son to a father : *Nolo*, 'I will not go.'

Here is no irresolute answer; no halting between two opinions, as the Jews did in the days of Elijah, betwixt God and Baal. No lukewarmness, as Laodicea, Rev. iii. 15 ; which was neither hot nor cold, and therefore in danger to be spewed up, as an offence to God's stomach. He is none of those *neuters*, that walk to heaven with statute legs. None of those fools, that onwards their journey to heaven stand in a quandary whether they should go forward to God or backwards to the world. He is not a tottering Israelite, but a plain Jezreelite ; straining his voice to the highest note of obstinacy : *Nolo*, 'I will not go.'

He was no hypocrite : here is no dissembling carriage of the business ; as if his father would be pleased with good words, or that terms smoother than Jacob could countenance rebellion rougher than Esau. He speaks his thought ; fall back, fall edge : 'I will not go.'

He was no lawyer, that is palpable : here be no demurs, nor pausing on an answer ; perhaps fearing a further solicitation, he goes roundly to work, and joins issue in a word : 'I will not go.'

He was no talkative fellow : that to every short question returns answer able to fill a volume ; with as many parentheses in one sentence as would serve Lipsius all his life. I have read of two sorts of ill answers. Come to one of them, and ask where his master is : he replies, He is not within ; and goes his way, not a word further. Demand so much of another : he answers, My master is gone to the Exchange, to talk with a merchant of Turkey, about the return of a ship which went out in April, laden with, &c. ; a voluble, tedious, headless, endless discourse. This son is one of the former ; he doth not trouble his father with many words : he is short with him, as if he wanted breath, or were loath to draw out the thread of his speech too long : *Nolo*, ' I will not go.'

He was no complimenter : he does not with a kissed hand, and cringing ham, practise his long-studied art of compliment ; and after a tedious antic of French courtesies, sets his tongue to a clinkant tune. No; he deals peremptorily, proudly, impudently, desperately : *Nolo*, ' I will not go' ; here is rebellion unmasking herself, and shewing her ugly visage to the world with an immodest impudence ; a protestation, a prostitution of the heart to all manner of impiety : *Nolo*, ' I will not go.'

You hear his answer : let us examine whether we can find any better comfort in the event. ' But he repented and went.'

THE TWO SONS

We say the second thoughts are most commonly the better. For all his big words, his stomach comes down. If I may take leave to gloss it, he could not want motives of humiliation to repentance, of excitation to obedience, if his recollected understanding did consider—(1) The person commanding; (2) The charge; (3) Himself, the party charged.

In this event, there is, first, a word of retraction; secondly, a word of reversion; thirdly, a word of proceeding. He was going on to hell roundly: this *but* interrupts him and stops his course. He begins in cool blood to pause and think upon it. His answer (and when he answered, his purpose) was, 'I will not go.' Yet here is a *but* that recollects him. After a little gathering up his spirits, and champing on this bit of the bridle that checked him, this *but*, he falls to be sorry for what he had spoken, and in direct terms to repentance. Lastly, when sorrow had well humbled him, and his wild spirits grew tame, he delays the time no longer, but falls instantly to his business: 'he went.' Faith taught him that his father was merciful, and would forgive his disobedient language, upon the true remorse of his conscience, especially when he came and found him 'working in the vineyard.'

But.—That which stops his lewd course is a

serious consideration of his folly. This *verunta-men*, like an oar, turns the boat another way, and saves him from the rock, and inevitable shipwreck, whereinto he was running his vessel. It is a gasp that recovers his swooning soul, when there was little hope of life left. He had died if this *but*, like a little *aqua vitæ*, had not fetched him back.

He repented.—They go far that never return. We heard this son at the highest stair of rebellion, now behold him descending by degrees : 'he repented and went.' Let this keep us from despairing of their salvation whom we see, for the present, given over to licentiousness. The prodigal returns home, the lost sheep is found, the dying thief is converted, this rebellious son is brought to repentance.

He went.—Sorrow for the evil past was not sufficient ; he must amend his future life. It is not enough to be sorry that he had loitered ; he must now labour in the vineyard.

Thus I have shewed you a precedent of repentance ; shew me a sinner that follows it : one Sabbath-breaker that offers to redeem God's holy time he hath abusively lost ; one encloser that will throw open his unjustly taken-in commons ; one extortioner that returns his thefts,—his usuries, I should say, but sure I did not mistake. We say,

We will not ; and indeed we do not. Repentance must not look in at our gates. We are not humbled to this day. God must lay us panting upon our bed of sickness, drink up our bloods, and raise our sins, like dust and smoke, in the eyes of our consciences, before we will be moved. Till then we bear our perjuries, blasphemies, oppressions, frauds, those unsupportable burdens, like cork and feathers upon our shoulders, without any sensible pressure. God touch our hearts, that we may 'repent, go and work in his vine-yard'!

We have done with the dissolute, and are fallen now upon the hypocrite. This second son hath also his charge; which because it is the same with the former, I lightly pass over. Only observe, that the Father commands every son to work. There must be no lazy ones in God's family. Adam, even in his innocency, Gen. ii. 15, was not permitted to sleep in the sweet bowers only, or to disport himself in the cool and pleasant walks, but he was bidden to dress the garden. But in the next chapter, when he had sinned, then labour was laid on him as a curse, chap. iii. 19. He and all his generations must earn their bread in the sweat of either brow or brain. There must be no ciphers in God's arithmetic, no mutes in his grammar, no blanks in his calendar, no dumb

shows on his stage, no false lights in his house, no
loiterers in his vineyard.

The charge of the father requires also this
son's answer: 'I go, sir.' He gives his father a
fair title, 'lord,' or 'sir,' as if he acknowledge to
him most submissive reverence; words soft as
butter, but the deeds of war are in the heart.
Many can give God good words, but saith the wise
philosopher appeal from their lips to their lives.
And you shall find these two differ, as it is seen
in some taverns: there are good sentences upon
the walls, Watch, Be sober, Fear God, &c., where
there is nothing but blasphemy, ebriety, and
unmeasurable rioting in the room. Our times
have lighted on a strange flashing zeal in the
tongue; but it is a poor fire of zeal that will not
make the pot of charity seethe. Our profession
is hot, but our hospitality cold. These men are
like a bad mill, that keeps a great clacking, but
grinds no grist. 'What hast thou to do to take
my covenant in thy mouth, seeing thou hatest
instruction in thy heart?' Ps. l. 16. The hen,
when she hath laid an egg, straight cackles it,
which causeth it instantly to be taken from her.
But here is one cackles when he has not laid,
and God coming, finds his nest empty. This is
to fry in words, freeze in deeds; to speak by ells,
and work by inches; to promise mountains, and

202

bring forth ridiculous mole-hills. A bad course and a good discourse agree not. Words are but vocal interpreters of the mind, actions real; what a man does we may be sure he thinks, not evermore what he says. Of the two, give me him that says little and doth much. Will you examine further who are like this son? They that can say here in the temple, 'Lord, hallowed be thy name'; scarce out of the church-doors, the first thing they do is to blaspheme it: that pray, 'Thy will be done,' when with all their powers they oppose it: and, 'Incline our hearts to keep thy laws,' when they utterly decline themselves. These are but devils in angels' feathers, stinking dunghills covered with white snow, rotten timber shining in the night; Pharisees' cups, *ignes fatui*, that seem to shine as fixed in the orb, yet are no other than crude substances and falling meteors. You hear how fairly this younger brother promiseth; what shall we find in the event? But 'he went not.'

What an excellent son had this been if his heart and tongue had been cut out of one piece! He comes on bravely, but, like an ill actor, he goes halting off. It is not profession, but obedience, that pleaseth God. 'Not every one that saith unto me, Lord, Lord, shall enter into heaven; but he that doth the will of my Father which is in heaven,' Matt. vii. 21. There are three things that cozen many, because they are preparatives to obedience, but are not it: Some intend well, as if the blast of a good meaning could blow them into heaven. Others prepare and set themselves in a towardness; but, like the George, booted and spurred, and on horseback, yet they stir not an inch. Others go a degree further, and they begin to think of a course for heaven: for a Sabbath or two you shall have them diligent churchmen; but the devil's in it, some vanity or other steals into their heart, and farewell devotion. All these are short, are nothing, may be worse than nothing; and it is only actual obedience that pleaseth God. Beloved, say no longer you will, but do; and the 'doer shall be blessed in his deed,' James i. 25. Which blessedness the mercies of God in Christ Jesus vouchsafe us! Amen.

THE SOUL'S SICKNESS

A Discourse—Divine, Moral, and Physical.

SICKNESSES in men's souls are bred like diseases in natural, or corruptions in civil bodies; with so insensible a progress, that they are not discerned till they be almost desperate. We can better brook our maladies than our remedies. In the head and other corporal parts there are many diseases, which I will not contend to find out; desiring only to slay, not all, but enough. I will borrow so much timber out of Galen's wood, as shall serve me for a scaffold to build up my moral discourse.

Headache and Brain-sickness.—Headache is diverse, say physicians, according to the causes: There is a headache called the megrim, *hemicrania*, possessing lightly one side of the head, and distinguished by a seam that runs along in the skull. There is a disease in the soul not unlike this, and they that labour of it are called brain-sick men. They may have some pretty understanding in part of their heads, but the other part is strangely sick of crotchets, singularities, and toyish inventions; wherein because they frolic themselves, they think all the world fools that admire them not. They are ever troubling themselves with unnecessary thoughtfulness of long or short, white or black, round or square; confounding their wits with geometrical dimensions, and studying of measure out of measure. A square cap on another man's head puts their head out of square, and they turn their brains into cotton with storming against a garment of linen. New Albutii, to moot the reasons, why if a cup fell down it brake; if a sponge, it brake not; why eagles fly, and not elephants. There be such students in the schools of Rome: what shall be done with an ass, if he get into the church, to the font uncovered, and drink the water of baptism. Upon the strange hap of a clerk's negligence, and a thirsty ass's entering the church, which are uncertain, they make themselves asses in certain. Or if a hungry mouse filch the body of our Lord, &c. Brave wits to invent mouse-traps. These curiosities in human, but much more in divine things, prove men brain-sick.

The cause of the megrim is the ascending of many vaporous humours, hot or cold, by the veins or arteries. The cause of this spiritual megrim, or brain-sickness, is the unkindly concurrence of

ignorance, arrogance, and affectation, like foggy
clouds, obscuring and smothering the true light
of their sober judgments; and bearing their
affections like a violent wind upon one only point
of the compass, new-fangled opinion : they hate
not to be observed, and had rather be notorious
than not notable. Opinion is a foot too much,
which spoils the verse. New physic may be
better than old, so may new philosophy; our
studies, observation, and experience perfecting
theirs; beginning, not at the Gamoth, as they did,
but, as it were, at the Ela : but hardly new
divinity; not that an ancient error should be
brought out against a new truth. A new truth !
Nay, an old newly come to light ; for error cannot
wage antiquity with truth. His desire is to be
cross to regularity ; and should he be enjoined a
hat, a cap would extremely please him ; were he
confined to extemporal and enthusiastical labours,
he would commend premeditation and study,
which now he abhors, because they are put on
him. He is unwise in being so bitter against
ceremonies ; for therein he is palpably against
himself, himself being nothing else but ceremony.
He loves not the beaten path ; and because every
fool, saith he, enters at the gate, he will climb
over the wall. Whiles the door of the church
stands open, he contends to creep through the

window, John x. 1. The brain-sick are no less than drunk with opinion; and that so strangely, that sleep, which helps other drunkards, doth them no good. Their ambitious singularity is often so violent that if it be not restrained it grows to a kind of frenzy, and so the megrim turns into the staggers. Herein, because we will not credit their positions, nor receive their crotchets in our set music, they reel into the Low Countries.

Inconstancy, a kind of Staggers.—There is a disease in the soul called inconstancy, not unfitly shadowed to us by a bodily infirmity, possessing the superior part of man—*vertigo*, a swimming in the head, a giddiness, or the staggers. The disease in the body is described to be an astonishing and dusking of the eyes and spirits, that the patient thinks all that he seeth to turn round, and is suddenly compassed with darkness. The parallel to it in the soul is inconstancy, a motion without rule, a various aspect, a diversifying intention. The inconstant man is like a Pourcontrell; if he should change his apparel so fast as his thought, how often in a day would he shift himself! He would be a Proteus too, and vary kinds. The reflection of every man's news melts him, whereof he is as soon glutted. As he is a noun, he is only adjective, depending on every novel persuasion; as a verb, he knows only the present tense. To-day he goes to the quay to be shipped for Rome, but before the tide come, his tide is turned. One party think him theirs, the adverse theirs : he is with both, with neither, not an hour with himself. Because the birds and beasts be at controversy, he will be a bat, and get him both wings and teeth. He would come to heaven, but for his halting : two opinions, like two watermen, almost pull him a-pieces, when he resolves to put his judgment into a boat, and go some whither ; presently he steps back, and goes with neither. It is a wonder if his affections, being but a little lukewarm water, do not make his religion stomach-sick. Indifference is his ballast, and opinion his sail : he resolves not to resolve. He knows not what he doth hold. He opens his mind to receive motions, as one opens his palm to take a handful of water—he hath very much, if he could hold it. He is sure to die, but not what religion to die in ; he demurs like a posed lawyer, as if delay could remove some impediments. He is drunk when he riseth, and reels in a morning fasting. He knows not whether he should say his *Pater noster* in Latin or English, and so leaves it and his prayers un-said. He makes himself ready for an appointed feast : by the way he hears of a sermon, he turns

thitherward ; yet betwixt the church gate and
church door he thinks of business, and retires
home again. In a controverted point he holds
with the last reasoner he either heard or read ; the
next diverts him ; and his opinion dwells with him
perhaps so long as the teacher of it is in his sight.
He will rather take dross for gold, than try it
in the furnace. He receives many judgments,
retains none, embracing so many faiths that he is
little better than an infidel. Thus his breast is
full of secret combats, contradictions, affirmations,
negatives ; and, whiles he refuseth to join with
others, he is divided in himself, and yet will rather
search excuses for his unstaidness, than ground
for his rest. He loathes manna after two days'
feeding, and is almost weary of the sun for perpetual shining. If the temple-pavements be ever
worn with his visitant feet, he will run far to a new
teacher ; and rather than be bound to his own
parish, he will turn recusant. He will admire a
new preacher till a quarter of the sand is out ; but
if the church doors be not locked up, he cannot
stay out the hour. What he promiseth to a
collection to-day, he forgets, or at least denies,
the next morning.

The signs of this disease in the body are a
mist and darkness coming upon every light
occasion. If he see a wheel turning round, or a

whirlpool, or any such circular motion, he is affected with giddiness. The symptoms of the spiritual staggers are semblable. He turns with those that turn, and is his neighbour's chameleon. He hates staidness as an earthen dulness. He prosecutes a business without fear or wit ; and rejecting the patience to consult, falls upon it with a peremptory heat : but like water once hot, is soonest frozen, and instantly he must shift his time and his place; neither is he so weary of every place, as every place is weary of him. He affects an object with dotage, and as superstitiously courts it as an idolater his gilded block. But it is a wonder if his passionate love outlive the age of a wonder—nine days. He respects in all things novelty above goodness ; and the child of his own brains within a week he is ready to judge a bastard. He salutes his wits after some invented toy, as a serving-man kisseth his hand ; when instantly on another plot arising, he kicks the former out of doors. He pulls down this day what he builded the other, now disliking the site, now the fashion, and sets men on work to his own undoing.

For the curing of this bodily infirmity many remedies are prescribed : odoriferous smells in weakness, the opening of a vein in better strength, cupping glasses applied to the hinder part of the

head, with scarification, gargarisms, and sternu-
tatory things together with setting the feet in hot
baths, &c. To cure this spiritual staggers, let the
patient be purged with repentance for his former
unsettledness; let him take an ounce of faith to
firm his brains; let his repose be on the Scriptures,
and thence fetch decision of all doubts; let a
skilful physician order him a good minister. Let
him stop his ears to rumours, and fix his eyes on
heaven, to be kept from distracting objects.
Let him keep the continual diet of prayer for the
Spirit of illumination; and thus he may be recovered.

Envy, a Consumption.—Envy fitly succeeds
anger, for it is nothing else but inveterate wrath.
The other was a frantic fit, and this is a consumption; a languishing disease in the body, the
beginning of dissolution, a broaching of the
vessel, not to be stopped till all the liquor of life is
run out. What the other tabe is in the body, I
list not to define, by reason that this spiritual sickness is a consumption of the flesh also, and a
pining away of the spirits; now since they both
have relation to the body, their comparison would
be confusion. Envy is the consumption I singularly
deal withal; which though I cannot cure, I will
hopefully minister to.

The cause of envy is others' prosperity, or

rather an evil eye shot upon it. The angry man
hath not himself, the envious must have no
neighbour. He battens at the maligned's misery ;
and if such a man riseth, he falls as if he were
planet-struck. I know not whether he could
endure to be in paradise with a superior. He
hates to be happy with any company. Envy sits
in a man's eyes, and wheresoever through those
windows it spies a blessing, it is sickness and
death unto it. He is even quarrelling with God
that his neighbour's field bears better corn, and
thinks himself poor if a near dweller be richer. He
will dispraise God's greatest blessings if they fall
besides himself, and grow sullen, so far as he dares,
with the prince that shall promote a better
deserver. There is no law perfect, if he was not at
the making it. He undertakes a great work, and
when he cannot accomplish it, he will give leave to
none other.

Idleness, the Lethargy.—Idleness in the soul
is a dangerous disease, as the lethargy in the
body. The very name of lethargy speaks the
nature, for it is compounded of λήθη, forgetfulness,
and ἀργὴς, slothful ; and so consequently is
defined to be a dull oblivion. The idle man is
a piece of base heavy earth, and moulded with
muddy and standing water. He lies in bed the
former half of the day, devising excuses to prevent

the afternoon's labour. He cannot endure to do anything by himself that may be done by attorney. He forestalls persuasion inducing him to any work, by forecasting the unprofitableness ; he holds business man's cruellest enemy, and a monstrous devourer of time. His body is so swollen with lazy humours, that he moves like a tun upon two pottle pots. He is tempted to covetise, for no other reason but to be able to keep servants ; whom he will rather trust than step out to oversee. Neither summer nor winter scape the blame of his laziness ; in the one it is too hot, in the other too cold, to work. Summer hath days too long, winter nights too cold ; he must needs help the one with a nap at noon, the other with a good fire. He was very fit to be a monk : spare him an early mass, and he will accept it ; yet howsoever, he will rather venture the censure than forsake a lazy calling.

The cause of the lethargy is abundant phlegm, overmuch cooling the brain, and thereby provoking sleep ; which putrefied in the brain, causeth a fever. The cause of idleness is indulgence to the flesh, a forgetfulness of the end of our creation, a wilful digression from man, for the lazy wretch is a dormouse in a human husk. To man motion is natural, the joints and eyes are made to move ; and the mind is never asleep, as if it were set to watch the body. Sleep is the image of death, saith the poet ; and therefore the church-sleeper is a dead corpse, set in his pew like a coffin, as if the preacher were to make his funeral sermon. He sings out harvest like the grasshopper ; therefore may at Christmas dance for and without his dinner. He riseth at noon to breakfast, which he falls to unwashed, and removes not out of his chair without a sleep. Whilst he sleeps, the enemy over-sows the field of his heart with tares. He is a patient subject for the devil to work on, a cushion for him.

Covetousness.—Our spiritual dropsy. Covetousness is a disease bred in the soul, through defect of faith and understanding. It properly resides in the inferior powers of the soul, the affections; but ariseth from the errors of the superior intellectual faculty : neither conceiving aright of God's all-sufficient help, nor of the world's all-deficient weakness.

Religion gives riches, and riches forget religion. Thus do our affections wheel about with an unconstant motion. Poverty makes us religious, religion rich, and riches irreligious. The covetous man is like a two-legged hog : whiles he lives, he is ever rooting in the earth, and never doth good till he is dead ; like a vermin, of no use till uncased. Himself is a monster, his life a riddle ; his face (and his heart) is prone to the ground ; his delight is to vex himself. It is a question whether he takes more care to get damnation, or to keep it ; and so is either a Laban or a Nabal, two infamous churls in the Old Testament, spelling one another's name backward. He keeps his god under lock and key, and sometimes, for the better safety, in his unclean vault. He is very eloquently powerful amongst his poor neighbours ; who, for awful fear, listen to Pluto as if he were Plato.

His heart is like the East Indian ground, where all the mines be so barren, that it bears neither grass, herb, plant, nor tree. The lightness of his purse gives him a heavy heart, which yet filled, doth fill him with more cares. His medicine is his malady ; he would quench his avarice with money, and this inflames it, as oil feeds the lamp, and some harish drinks increase thirst. His proctor in the law, and protector against the law, is his money. His alchemy is excellent, he can project much silver, and waste none in smoke. His rhetoric is how to keep him out of the subsidy. His logic is to prove heaven in his chest. His mathematics, to measure the goodness of anything by his own profit. His arithmetic is in addition and multiplication, much in subtraction, nothing in division. His physic is to minister gold to his

eye, though he starve his body. *Sculptura* is his
Scriptura ; and he hath so many gods as images
of coin. He is an ill harvest-man, for he is all at
the rake, nothing at the pitchfork. The devil is
a slave to God, the world to the devil, the covetous
man to the world; he is a slave to the devil's slave,
so that his servant is like to have a good office.
He foolishly buries his soul in his chest of silver,
when his body must be buried in the mould of
corruption. When the fisher offers to catch him
with the net of the gospel, he strikes into the mud
of avarice, and will not be taken. He sells his
best grain, and feeds himself on mouldy crusts ;
he returns from plough, if he remembers that his
cupboard was left unlocked. If once in a reign
he invites his neighbours to dinner, he whiles the
times with frivolous discourses, to hinder feeding ;
sets away the best dish, affirming it will be better
cold ; observes how much each guest eateth, and
when they are risen and gone, falleth to himself,
what for anger and hunger, with a sharp appetite.
If he smells of gentility, you shall have at the
nether end of his board a great pasty uncut up,
for it is filled with bare bones : somewhat for show,
but most to keep the nether mess from eating. He
hath sworn to die in debt to his belly. He deducts
from a servant's wages the price of a halter, which
he cut to save his master, when he had hung him-

self at the fall of the market. He lends nothing,
nor returns borrowed, unless it be sent for;
which if he cannot deny, he will delay, in hope to
have it forgotten. To excuse his base and sordid
apparel, he commends the thriftiness of King
Henry, how cheap his clothes were. His fist is
like the prentice's earthen box, which receives all,
but lets out nothing till it be broken. He is in
more danger to be sand-blind than a goldsmith.
Therefore some call him *avidum, à non videndo.*
He must rise in the night with a candle to see his
corn, though he stumble in the straw, and fire his
barn. He hath a lease of his wits, during the
continuance of his riches : if any cross starts away
them, he is mad instantly. He would slay an ass
for his skin ; and, like Hermocrates dying,
bequeath his own goods to himself. His case is
worse than the prodigal's; for the prodigal shall
have nothing hereafter, but the covetous hath
nothing in present.

Pride and the Pleurisy.—The pleurisy is defined
to be an inward inflammation ; Pride is a pursy
affection of the soul without law, for it is rebellious;
without measure, for it delights in extremes ; without reason, for it doth all things with precipitation.
The proud man is bitten of the mad dog, the
flatterer, and so runs on a garget. This spiritual
disease ariseth from a blown opinion of one's self:

which opinion is either from ignorance of his own emptiness, and so, like a tumbler full of nothing but air, makes a greater sound than a vessel of precious liquor ; or from arrogance of some good, which the owner knows too well. He never looks short of himself, but always beyond the mark, and offers to shoot further than he looks ; but ever falls two bows short—humility and discretion.

The symptoms of the pleurisy are difficult breathing, a continual fever, a vehement prickling on the affected side. The proud man is known by his gait, which is peripatetical, strutting like some new churchwarden. He thinks himself singularly wise, but his opinion is singular, and goes alone. In the company of good wits, he fenceth in his ignorance with the hedge of silence, that observation may not climb over to see his follies. He would have his judgment for wearing his apparel pass unmended, not uncommended. He shifts his attire on some solemn day, twice at least in twelve hours ; but cannot shift himself out of the mercer's books once in twelve months. His greatest envy is the next gentleman's better clothes ; which if he cannot better or equalise, he wears his own neglected. His apparel carries him to church without devotion ; and he riseth up at the Creed to join with the rest in confession, not of his faith, but his pride; for sitting down hides much of his bravery. He feeds with no cheerful stomach, if he sit not at the upper end of the table and be called young master; where he is content to rise hungry, so the observant company weary him with drinking to: on this condition he gives his obligation for the shot. He loves his lying glass beyond any true friend; and tells his credulous auditors how many gentlewomen have run mad for him, when if a base female servant should court him, I dare wager he proves no *Adonis*.

This fault is well mended when a man is well minded,—that is, when he esteems of others better than himself. Otherwise a proud man is like the rising earth in mountainous places: this swells up *monte*, as he *mente*; and the more either earth advanceth itself, perpetually they are the more barren. He lives at a high sail, that the puffy praises of his neighbours may blow him into the enchanted island, vainglory. He shines like a glowworm in a dark village, but is a crude thing when he comes to the court. If the plethora swells him in the vein of valour, nothing but well-beating can hold him to a man. If ever he goes drunk into the field, and comes off with a victorious parley, he would swell to a son of Anak.

THE SOUL'S SICKNESS

Palsy and Timorous Suspicion.—The former sick were *tumidi*, these are *timidi*; they were bold to all evil, these are fearful to all good. This spiritual disease is a cowardly fearfulness and a distrustful suspicion both of actions and men.

The signs of the palsy are manifest; of this not very close and reserved. He conceives what is good to be done, but fancies difficulties and dangers, like to knots in a bulrush, or rubs in a smooth way. He would bowl well at the mark of integrity, if he durst venture it. He hath no journey to go, but either there are bugs, or he imagines them. Had he a pardon for his brother, (being in danger of death,) and a hare should cross him in the way, he would no further, though his brother hanged for it. He owes God some good-will, but he dares not shew it. When a poor plaintiff calls him for a witness, he dares not reveal the truth, lest he offend the great adversary. He is a new Nicodemus, and would steal to heaven if nobody might see him. He makes a good motion bad by his fearfulness and doubting ; and he calls his trembling by the name of conscience. He is like that collier, that passing through Smithfield, and seeing some on the one side hanging, he demands the cause ; answer was made, for denying the supremacy to King Henry : on the other side some burning, he asks the cause ; answered, for denying the real presence in the sacrament : Some, quoth he, hanged for Papistry, and some burned for Protestancy ? Then hoit on, a God's name : I'll be neither. His religion is primarily his prince's, subordinately his landlord's. Neither deliberates he more to take a new religion, to rise by it, than he fears to keep his old, lest he fall by it. All his care is for a *ne noceat*. He is a busy inquirer of all Parliament acts, and quakes as they are read, lest he be found guilty. He is sick, and afraid to die, yet holds the potion in a trembling hand, and quakes to drink his recovery. His thoughts are an ill balance, and will never be equally poised. He is a light vessel, and every great man's puff is ready to overturn him. Whiles Christ stands on the battlements of heaven, and beckons him thither by his word, his heart answers, I would fain be there, but that some troubles stand in my way. He would ill with Peter walk to him on the pavement of the sea, or thrust out his hand with Moses, to take up a crawling serpent, or hazard the loss of himself to find his Saviour. His mind is ever in suspicion, in suspension, and dares not give a confident determination either way. Resolution and his heart are utter enemies ; and all his philosophy is to be a sceptic. Whether is worse, to do an evil action with resolution that it is good, or a

good action with dubitation that it is evil, some-
body tell me. I am sure neither is well, for an
evil deed is evil, whatsoever the agent think ; and
for the other, 'Whatsoever is not of faith is sin.'
Negatively, this rule is certain and infallible : ' It
is good to forbear the doing of that which we are
not sure is lawful to be done.' Affirmatively, the
work being good, labour thy understanding so to
think it.

Immoderate Thirst and Ambition.—There is a
disease in the body called immoderate thirst ;
which is after much drinking, desired and
answered, a still sensible dryness. By this I
would (I suppose, not unfitly) express that spiritual
disease, ambition,—a proud soul's thirst, when a
draught of honour causeth a drought of honour ;
and like Tully's strange soil, much rain of promotion falling from his heaven, the court, makes
him still as dry as dust. He is a most rank churl,
for he drinks often, and yet would have no man
pledge him.

The signs of the disease are best discerned by
the patient's words. The cause of ambition is a
strong opinion of honour ; how well he could
become a high place, or a high place him.
He professeth a new quality, called the art of
climbing ; wherein he teacheth others by pattern,
not so much to aspire, as to break their necks.

223

No stair pleaseth him if there be a higher;
and yet, ascended to the top, he complains of
lowness. He is not so soon laid in his bed of
honour but he dreams of a higher preferment, and
would not sit on a seat long enough to make it
warm. His advancement gives him a fresh
provocation, and he now treads on that with a
disdainful foot, which erewhile he would have
kissed to obtain. He climbs falling towers, and
the hope to scale them swallows all fear of
toppling down. He is himself an intelligencer to
greatness, yet not without under-officers of the
same rank. You shall see him narrow-eyed with
watching, affable and open-breasted like Absalom,
full of insinuation so long as he is at the stair-
foot; but when authority hath once spoken kindly
to him, with 'Friend, sit up higher,' he looks
rougher than Hercules; so big as if the river of
his blood would not be banked within his veins.
Like a great wind, he blows down all friends that
stand in his way to rising. Policy is his post-
horse, and he rides all upon the spur, till he come
to Nonesuch. His greatest plague is a rival.

He is a child in his gaudy desires, and great
titles are his rattles, which still his crying till he
see a new toy. He kisses his wits, as a courtier
his hand, when any wished fortune salutes him;
and it tickles him that he hath stolen to promotion

without God's knowledge. Ambition is the rack
whereon he tortureth himself. The court is the
sea wherein he desires to fish ; but the net of his
wit and hope breaks, and there he drowns himself.
To cure the immoderate thirst of ambition, let
him take from God this prescript : 'He that
exalteth himself shall be brought low ; but he that
humbleth himself shall be exalted.' That he who
sets himself down in the lower room hears the
master of the feast's invitation, 'Friend, sit up
higher.' That the first step to heaven's court is
humility : Matt. v. 3, 'Blessed are the poor in
spirit, for theirs is the kingdom of heaven.' That
he who walks on plain ground is in little danger
to fall ; if he do fall, he riseth with small hurt ;
but he that climbs high is in more danger of
falling, and if he fall, of killing. That the great
blasts of powerful envy overthrow oaks and cedars,
that oppose their huge bodies, and pass through
hollow willows, or over little shrubs, that grow
under the wall. That the honours of this world
have no satisfactory validity in them. The poor
labourer would be a farmer ; the farmer, after two
or three dear years, aspires to a yeoman ; the
yeoman's son must be a gentleman. The gentleman's ambition flies justice-height. He is out of
square with being a squire, and shoots at knight-
hood. Once knighted, his dignity is nothing,

except worth a noble title. This is not enough, the world must count him a count, or he is not satisfied. He is weary of his earldom, if there be a duke in the land. That granted, he thinks it base to be a subject ; nothing now contents him but a crown. Crowned, he vilifies his own kingdom for narrow bounds, whiles he hath greater neighbours ; he must be Cæsared to a universal monarch. Let it be granted, is he yet content? No ; then the earth is a molehill, too narrow for his mind, and he is angry for lack of elbow-room.

The Putrid Fever, or Hypocrisy.—For the signs of this fever they be not externally discerned. The hypocrite is exceedingly rotten at core, like a Sodom apple, though an ignorant passenger may take him for sound. He looks squint-eyed, aiming at two things at once : the satisfying his own lusts, and that the world may not be aware of it. He is on Sunday like the Rubric, or Sunday-letter, zealously red ; but all the week you may write his deeds in black. He fries in words, freezeth in works ; speaks by ells, doth good by inches. He is a rotten tinder, shining in the night : an *ignis fatuus*, looking like a fixed star ; a 'painted sepulchre,' that conceals much rottenness ; a crude glowworm shining in the dark ; a stinking dunghill covered over with snow ; a fellow of a bad course, and good discourse; a loose-hung mill, that keeps great clacking, but grinds no grist; a lying hen, that cackles when she hath not laid. He is like some tap-house that hath upon the painted walls written, 'Fear God, be sober, watch and pray,' &c., when there is nothing but swearing and drunkenness in the house. His tongue is hot as if he had eaten pepper, which works coldly at the heart. He burns in the show of forward profession; but it is a poor fire of zeal, that will not make the pot of charity seethe. He is in company holy and demure, but alone demurs of the matter; so shuts out the devil at the gate, and lets him in at the postern.

His words are precise, his deeds concise; he prays so long in the church, that he may with less suspicion prey on the church; which he doth the more peremptorily, if his power be answerable. If his place will afford it, his grace will without question. He bears an earnest affection to the temple, as a hungry man to his meat, only to devour it. Some are so charitable, that having got the tithe-corn from the church, they reserve from the presented incumbent their petty tithes also; like monstrous thieves, that having stole the whole piece, ask for the remnants. Nay, it is not enough that they devour our parsonages, but they also devour our persons with their contumelious slanders. Advantage can make his religion play at fast and loose, for he only so long grows full of devotion, as he may grow full by devotion. His arguments are weak or strong, according to his cheer; and he discourses best after dinner. Self-conceit swells him, and popular applause bursts him. He never gives the law good words but when it hath him upon the hip. Like a kind hen, he feeds his chickens fat, starves himself. He forceth formal preciseness, like a porter, to hold the door, whiles devils dance within. He gives God nothing but show, as if he would pay him his reckoning with chalk; which increaseth the debt. If ever his alms smell of bounty, he gives them in public. He that desires more to be seen of men than of God commend me to his conscience by this token, he is a hypocrite. He is false in his friendship, heartless in his zeal, proud in his humility. He rails against interludes, yet is himself never off the stage; and condemns a mask, when his whole life is nothing else. He sends a beggar from his gate bountifully feasted with Scripture sentences; and (though he likes them not) so much of the statutes as will serve to save his money. But if every one were of his profession, charity's hand would no longer hold up poverty's head. What his tongue spoke, his hands recant; and he weeps when he talks of his youth, not that it was wicked, but that it is not. His tongue is his dissimulation's lacquey, and runs continually on that errand : he is the stranger's saint, his neighbour's sycophant, his own politician ; his whole life being nothing else but a continual scribbling after the set copy of hypocrisy.

Vainglory.—You shall easily know a vainglorious man. He stands so pertly, that you may know he is not laden with fruit. If you would drink of his wisdom, knock by a sober question at the barrel, and you shall find by the sound his wits are empty. In all companies, like chaff, he will be uppermost ; he is some surfeit in nature's stomach, and cannot be kept down. A goodly cypress tree, fertile only of leaves. He drinks to none beneath the salt; and it is his grammar-rule without exception, not to confer with an inferior in public. His impudence will overrule his ignorance to talk of learned principles, which come from him like a treble part in a bass voice, too big for it. Living in some under-stair office, when he would visit the country, he borrows some gallant's cast suit of his servant, and therein, player-like, acts that part among his besotted neighbours. When he rides his master's great horse out of ken, he vaunts of him as his own, and brags how much he cost him. He feeds upon others' courtesy, others' meat ; and (whether more?) either fats him. At his inn he calls for chickens at spring, and such things as cannot be had; whereat angry, he sups, according to his purse, with a red herring. Far enough from knowledge, he talks of his castle, (which is either in the air, or enchanted,) of his lands, which are some pastures in the fairy-ground, invisible, nowhere. He offers to purchase lordships, but wants money for the earnest. He makes others' praises as introductions to his own, which must transcend; and calls for wine, that he may make known his rare vessel of deal at home : not forgetting to tell you, that a Dutch merchant sent it him for some extraordinary desert. He is a wonder everywhere : among fools for his bravery, among wise men for his folly. He loves a herald for a new coat, and hires him to lie upon his pedigree. All nobility, that is ancient, is of his alliance; and the great man is but of the first head, that doth not call him cousin. In his hall, you shall see an old rusty sword hung up, which he swears killed Glendower in the hands of his grandsire. He fathers upon himself some villanies, because they are in fashion; and so vilifies his credit to advance it. If a new famous courtezan be mentioned, he deeply knows her ; whom indeed he never saw. He will be ignorant of nothing, though it be a shame to know it. His barrel hath a continual spigot, but no tunnel; and like an unthrift, he spends more than he gets. His speech of himself is ever historical, histrionical. He is indeed admiration's creature, and a circumstantial mountebank.

The Busybody moots more questions in an hour than the seven wise men could resolve in seven years. There is a kind of down or curdle on his wit, which is like a gentlewoman's train, more than needs. He would sing well, but that he is so full of crotchets. His questions are like a plume of feathers, which fools would give anything for, wise men nothing. He hath a greater desire to know where hell is, than to scape it; to know what God did before he made the world, than what he will do with him when it is ended; his neighbours' estate to a penny and wherein he fails he supplies by intelligence from their flattered servants: he would serve well for an informer to the subsidy-book. He delays every passenger with inquiry of news; and because the country cannot satiate him, he travels every term to London for it: whence returning without his full load, himself makes it up by the way. He buys letters from the great city with capons; which he wears out in three days, with perpetual opening them to his companions. If he hears but a word of some state act, he professeth to know it and the intention, as

231

if he had been of the council. He hears a lie in private, and hastes to publish it; so one knave gulls him, he innumerable fools, with the 'strange fish at Yarmouth,' or the 'serpent in Sussex.' He can keep no secret in, without the hazard of his buttons. He loves no man a moment longer than either he will tell him, or hear of him, news. If the spirit of his tongue be once raised, all the company cannot conjure it down. He teaches his neighbour to work unsent for, and tells him of some dangers without thanks. He comments upon every action, and answers a question ere it be half propounded. Alcibiades having purchased a dog at an unreasonable price, cut off his tail, and let him run about Athens; whiles every man wondered at his intent, he answered that his intent was their wonder, for he did it only to be talked of. The same author reports the like of a gawish traveller that came to Sparta, who standing in the presence of Lacon a long time upon one leg, that he might be observed and admired, cried at the last, 'O Lacon, thou canst not stand so long upon one leg.' 'True,' said Lacon; 'but every goose can.'

Flattery.—The main cause of flattery is a kind of self-love : for he only commends others to mend himself. The *communis terminus*, where all his frauds, dissimulations, false phrases and praises, his admirations and superlative titles, meet, is his purse. His tongue serves two masters, his great one's ear, his own avarice.

He is after the nature of a barber ; and first trims the head of his master's humour, and then sprinkles it with court-water. He scrapes out his diet in courtesies ; and cringeth to his glorious object, as a little cur to a mastiff, licking his hand, not with a healing, but poisoning tongue. Riches make many friends : truly, they are friends to the riches, not to the rich man. A great proud man, because he is admired of a number of hang-byes, thinks he hath many friends. So the ass that carried the goddess thought all the knees bowed to her, when they reverenced her burden. They play like flies in his beams, whiles his wealth warms them. Whilst, like some great oak, he stands high and spreads far in the forest, in-numerable beasts shelter themselves under him, feeding like hogs on his acorns ; but when the axe of distress begins to fell him, there is not one left to hinder the blow. Like burrs, they stick no longer on his coat than there is a nap on it. These kites would not flock to him, but that he is a fat carcase. Sejanus, whom the Romans worship in the morning as a semigod, before night they tear a-pieces. Even now stoops, and presently strokes. You may be sure he is but a gallipot, full of honey, that these wasps hover about ; and when they have fed themselves at his cost, they give him a sting for his kindness.

The flatterer is young gallants' schoolmaster, and enters them into book learning. Your cheating tradesman can no more be without such a factor than a usurer without a broker. The fox in the fable, seeing the crow highly perched, with a good morsel in his mouth, flattered him that he sung well, with no scant commendations of his voice; whereof the crow proud, began to make a noise, and let the meat fall : the foolish bird seeing now himself deceived, soon left singing, and the fox fell to eating. I need not moral it. The instrument, his tongue, is tuned to another's ear; but, like a common fiddler, he dares not sing an honest song. He lifts up his patron at the tongue's end, and sets him in a superlative height; like a Pharos, or the eye of the country, when he is indeed the eye-sore. He swears to him that his commending any man is above a justice of peace's letter, and that the eyes of the parish wait upon him for his grace. He insinuates his praise, most from others' report; wherein, very rankly, he wrongs three at once; he belies the named commender; the person to whom this commendation is sent; and most of all himself, the messenger. Whilst he supplies a man with the oil of flattery, he wounds his heart; like thunder, which breaks the bone without scratching the skin. He seldom speaks so pompously of his friend, except he be sure of porters to carry it him. He is the proud man's earwig, and having once gotten in, imposthumes his head.

Conclusion.—Innumerable are the body's infirmities : *introitus unus, innumeri exitus,* there being but one means of coming into the world, infinite of going out; and sickness is death's liege ambassador. But they are few and scant, if compared to the soul's, which being a better piece of timber, hath the more teredines breeding in it; as the fairest flower hath the most cantharides attending on it.

There be three things, say physicians, that grieve the body :—First, the cause of sickness, a contranatural distemper, which lightly men bring on themselves, though the sediments rest in our sin-corrupted nature. Secondly, sickness itself. Thirdly, the coincidents that either fellow it or follow it. In the soul there be three grievances:— First, original pravity, a natural ἀνομία—proclivity to evil, contradiction to good. Secondly, actual sin, the main sickness. Thirdly, the concomitant effects, which are punishments corporal and spiritual, temporal and eternal. For all sin makes work, either for Christ or Satan : for Christ, to expiate by his blood, and the efficacy of that once-performed, ever available passion; or for the devil, as God's executioner to plague. Many remedies are given for many diseases; the sum is this—the best physician is Christ Jesus, the best physic the Scriptures. Ply the one, fly to the other. Let this teach thee, he must cure thee: that 'express image of his Father's person, and brightness of his glory,' Heb. i. 3, in whom the graces of God shine without measure. Oft have you seen in one heaven many stars; behold in this sun, as in one star, many heavens; for 'in him dwelleth all fulness,' Col. i. 19. Let us fly by our faithful prayers to this physician, and entreat him for that medicine that issued out of his side, 'water and blood,' to cure all our spiritual maladies. And when in mercy he hath cured us, let our diet be a conversation led after the canon of his sacred truth; that whatsoever become of this frail vessel, our flesh, floating on the waves of this world, the passenger, our soul, may be saved in the day of the Lord Jesus. Amen.